PREPARING
for a
KINGDOM
MARRIAGE

PREPARING
for a
KINGDOM MARRIAGE
TONY EVANS

A COUPLE'S WORKBOOK TO
CONNECTING WITH GOD'S PURPOSE

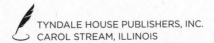

TYNDALE HOUSE PUBLISHERS, INC.
CAROL STREAM, ILLINOIS

FOCUS ON THE FAMILY | FOCUS ON MARRIAGE™

CONTENTS

INTRODUCTION

✤✤✤✤✤✤

WELCOME TO *PREPARING FOR A KINGDOM MARRIAGE*. We are so excited that you and your future spouse are taking the time to prepare for this monumental decision and transition in your life! Your marriage will be the foundation for your future, in more ways than you can even imagine. That's why we've put together this workbook to help you open up the lines of dialogue and expand your thinking on some of the more critical aspects needed to turn your *vow* into *wow*! It is my desire that your marriage will be the single most rewarding, satisfying, and encouraging area of your entire life. When that is true, there's no telling how God will use you both as individuals and as a couple for His purposes and His glory.

A few pointers as we start our time together. This workbook is intended to be used alongside my book *Kingdom Marriage*. Now, keep in mind, *Kingdom Marriage* is written to couples who are already married. So as you read it, you may need to look ahead into your relationship a bit through forecasting, or take my word for it if it's something you can't even imagine you and your partner one day doing (like arguing!). Each lesson coincides with a chapter in *Kingdom Marriage*, so be sure to read that chapter prior to watching the video segment or doing the personal and couple reflection and lesson questions.

In addition, we've put together several appendixes, three of them for you to use *before* you start your time in this study. These appendixes go into some discovery aspects about you and your partner that will be helpful information and a framework for moving through these lessons. We cover things such as communication, personality, spiritual gifts, purpose, mission, and vision statements—and even your own couple's logo!

In Appendix C there is a list of service opportunities. Read through them together and choose which one(s) fit your schedule, the needs of those around you, and your interests. You can choose one or you can do all of them. It is entirely up to you. What we want you to do, though, is to serve somewhere every single week of this study, beginning this week. Your oneness will develop organically as a couple when you serve others together. So look over that appendix before you start lesson 1.

Appendix D includes a chapter from my book *Raising Kingdom Kids*, in which I talk about the very common occurrence of blended families. If one or both of you already have children, please take the time to read this appendix. I also want to encourage you to view the study questions and lessons through the grid of your entire family, not solely your new marriage, as you go through each week.

Appendix E provides a home budget template to use with lesson 10. And Appendix F offers coaching for mentors working with engaged couples.

Each week's lesson gives you some time to review the reading material, go deeper in personal application and Bible study, discuss what you are learning, and meet with a mentor or mentoring couple who can serve as guides. It is my desire that as you both move toward your wedding day, you will experience God's supernatural hand of alignment, unity, and love drawing you together at a level deeper than you even imagined possible.

Marriage truly is the greatest gift given to us on earth. Cherish it and honor it by preparing wisely for it.

Cheering for you,

Tony Evans

VIDEO LINKS INFORMATION

❖❖❖❖❖❖

AS YOU BEGIN to use the thirteen lessons in this workbook, you'll see that the first part of each lesson is the "Time with Tony Video Segment." These are brief videos in which I introduce the subject of that lesson and encourage you in your study. I hope this personal touch will convey to you and your intended how much I care about you and the success of your approaching marriage.

These videos are part of the program and are provided at no extra charge. To access them, simply go to FocusOnTheFamily.com/MarriagePrep, enter a little information about yourself, and enjoy!

❖❖❖❖❖❖

PART I

The Foundation of a

KINGDOM MARRIAGE

LESSON 1

✤✤✤✤✤✤

ORIGIN

Section 1: *Time with Tony Video Segment*

Begin your time together by opening in prayer, then watch the lesson 1 video segment. (See page ix for link.)

Section 2: *Study Time*

Heart Highlights

Read chapter 1 of *Kingdom Marriage* individually. Rewrite the following highlights from the chapter in your own words, or, if you prefer, simply reword the statements in a conversation you have with your fiancé at a later time. Make sure to write them or speak them in such a way that they will personally apply to you and your future spouse.

1. The foundation of civilization is the family, and the foundation of the family is marriage; therefore, the destruction of marriage naturally results in the destruction of civilization. This is why it is critical that we make strengthening marriages and families an integral part of our lives.

2. The number one way to bring God glory is through surrender to His sovereign rule. This acknowledges His supremacy over every area of life. When we operate our marriages based on these principles of the kingdom agenda, we are free to experience God's hand of blessing and His promise to work all things together for good (Romans 8:28).

3. The reason so many of us as believers are struggling in our marriages is that we want God to bless our agenda for our relationship rather than us fulfilling His agenda. We want God to okay our plans rather than our fulfilling His. We want God to bring us glory rather than us bringing Him glory through honoring the marriage covenant as He intended it.

4. Happiness is to be a benefit of a strong marriage, but not the goal. The goal is the reflection of God through the advancement of His kingdom on earth. Happiness occurs as an organic outgrowth when this goal is sought.

5. Kingdom couples must view marriage through God's kingdom lens. Marriage is a covenantal union designed by God in order to strengthen the capacity of each partner to carry out His plan in their lives.

Digging Deeper

1. Read Psalm 103:19. In what ways does an earthly king receive allegiance and obedience from those he rules? Compare and contrast how God should receive our allegiance and obedience in all that we think, say, or do.

2. Read Genesis 1:26-28 and Psalm 8:3-6. What does it mean to "rule" on behalf of God's kingdom authority on earth? Describe what "managerial responsibility" looks like as stewards of God's resources such as your time, talents, and treasures.

3. Keeping in mind Philippians 4:13, list the potential areas of your upcoming marriage that are impossible to fix or work out within your own power.

4. In what way does Matthew 19:6 address issues of priorities in a marriage?

5. First Corinthians 7:4 is not a license to control or dominate each other in a marriage. Describe what is meant in this passage and how this verse can and should be honored in your relationship as a married couple.

SECTION 3: *Personal Time*

For this reason a man shall leave his father and his mother, and be joined to his wife; and they shall become one flesh.
GENESIS 2:24

You and I can't improve on God's idea for anything. God created the covenant of marriage, so we will have greater power and greater pleasure in our marriages when we follow His plan. The foundational thought of marriage is simple: leave, join, and become one. Notice the reason for the closeness of the marriage union according to Genesis 2:23-24. A man is to join himself totally to his wife "for this reason," because woman "was taken out of Man" (verse 23). Woman came from man's flesh; thus a man and wife are to become one flesh *again*.

The tragedy today is that a lot of people have these words read at their weddings, but they don't know all that is involved. In particular, too many young people who get married have not really left their parents emotionally, and even at times financially.

Ask yourselves: Is your mate a nice *addition* to your life, or is he or she your *life*?

When you are married, you must be willing to place second in your life anything or anyone that seeks to be more important than your spouse. Now, that doesn't mean you sit around all day and look into each other's eyes. No, but it does mean that your priority shifts to making the needs of your spouse more important than the needs and demands of other things in your life, outside of God Himself.

Reflect & Respond

Spend a few moments discussing with your fiancé the answers to the following questions based on this week's devotional thought.

1. In your own words, what does it mean that "a man shall leave his father and his mother"?

2. What are some ways people do not leave their parents when they get married, and how can that prove to be detrimental to their marriage relationship?

3. Think about and share who/what you feel will be the most challenging person(s) or thing(s) for you to place beneath the priority of your new marriage. (Note: It may not be your parents. It could be a friend, job, dream, hobby.)

4. Discuss why or how this could be a challenge to you. What has this particular commitment meant to you in the past?

5. Come up with ways to hold each other accountable to the priority of the marriage relationship, in light of other commitments and attachments in your life. Give yourselves freedom to remind each other of the priority of your marriage in a non-controlling, respectful way.

SECTION 4: *Take-It-In Time*

Mentor Moment

Couples who stick together understand that marriage is a sacred and solemn mystery in the eyes of God. As a result, they enter the relationship with the attitude that *divorce is not an option*. They understand that marriage is a life-long *adventure*, filled with triumphs and defeats. Like Jesus, "who for the joy set before Him endured the cross, despising the shame" (Hebrews 12:2), they press on toward the goal in both good times and bad.

1. If you had to define "marriage," what words would you use? What makes marriage unique and different from any other human relationship?

2. How would you describe your "long view" of your relationship? Where do you see yourselves in five years? Ten years? Twenty?

3. When you run into obstacles, roadblocks, or conflicts in your marriage, what will be your "default" reaction? Will you get angry? Run home to Mother? Blame one another? Or will you look for ways to solve the problems and move forward?

4. Did you see lifelong commitment modeled in your family of origin? How has your experience affected your view of this concept? In the Marine Corps they say, "When the going gets tough, the tough get going." Does this maxim apply to marriage? If so, how? Would you describe your future marriage as an adventure? Would you like to make it *more* adventurous? If so, how?

5. The Bible says, "A man shall leave his father and his mother, and be joined to his wife; and they shall become one flesh" (Genesis 2:24). What do you think it means to be "one flesh"?

SECTION 5: *Time Together*

Date Night Discussion

Summary Statements: Set aside time to explore the following summary statements and reflection questions in the context of a date or while sharing a meal. Open your discussion time in prayer, asking the Lord to draw you both together in alignment under Him. Begin by reading these foundational principles aloud to each other. Afterward, discuss what they mean to you personally and how you want them to be displayed in your marriage. Finally, discuss the Talking Topics that follow the foundational principles.

- The kingdom agenda is the visible manifestation of the comprehensive rule of God over every area of life.

- Every thought, word, or action in our marriage must align itself under God's rule and within His will and purpose for our lives, both individually and together as one.

- Our marriage shares a mission, not just our emotions.

Talking Topics: Take time to discuss what you believe is your personal calling. If you do not yet know your calling, discuss what your gifts, skills, experiences, passions, and interests are and how those may intersect in bringing glory to God. Share how you hope that your marriage will strengthen each of your individual callings and purposes, and if there are any points of convergence in your callings where they could be carried out together.

LESSON 2

✤✤✤✤✤✤

ORDER

SECTION 1: *Time with Tony Video Segment*

Begin your time together by opening in prayer, then watch the lesson 2 video segment. (See page ix for link.)

SECTION 2: *Study Time*

Heart Highlights

Read chapter 2 of *Kingdom Marriage* individually. Rewrite the following highlights from the chapter in your own words, or, if you prefer, simply reword the statements in a conversation you have with your fiancé at a later time. Make sure to write them or speak them in such a way that they will personally apply to you and your future spouse.

1. Without order there is chaos. This is why Satan continually tries to stir things up in our marriages so that we can never progress to that place of order, peace, harmony, and progress.

2. God has ordained a rulership for you and your spouse to carry out. He has intentionally brought the two of you together in order to fulfill His purpose for your lives. Yet, just as you wouldn't be able to drive in rush-hour traffic without the establishment of and adherence to lanes, neither can you move forward to carry out all God has in store for you as a couple without the lanes of His prescribed order. Satan knows that if he is going to cancel out your capacity to rule, he has to disrupt order by creating dissension and division. Whatever Satan can divide he can control. Especially your marriage.

3. If you will commit to applying God's prescribed order to your marriage relationship, you will begin to see the fruit of blessing showing up not only in your partnership, but also within other areas connected to your family. This is because you will open up the opportunity for greater favor to flow.

4. If a husband desires his wife to be answerable to him, she should also see that modeled in him as being answerable to Christ. What far too many men do is get out of their lane in respect to Christ but still expect their wives to be in their lanes with respect to them. No one should be shocked if a marriage ends in disarray if a man is not operating according to the principles of God. He's out of his lane.

5. As we see from Adam and Eve, when headship is broken, authority is lost. Without spiritual authority, it is difficult to accomplish anything worthwhile, let alone experience a thriving marriage.

Digging Deeper

1. Look up 1 Corinthians 11:3. Share how this passage makes you feel. In what way does it evoke positive emotions, and in what way (if any) does it evoke negative emotions?

2. Read Matthew 8:5-10. In what way does order provide an opportunity for kingdom authority to take place? Describe some examples you have seen, taken part in, or heard about where respecting roles brought about a better result. (For example: airline pilots, a drama play, the education system).

3. Based on 1 Corinthians 11:8-12, what does it mean when the "symbol of authority" over a woman is there "because of the angels"?

4. What action does Jesus refer to in Matthew 11:29? Describe how this action would impact your choices and decisions (if literally done)? What does Jesus promise for those who choose to surrender to His rule in their lives?

5. Compare 1 Peter 3:5 with James 4:10. In whom do you place your trust when you willingly choose to surrender your will before another? And what can you anticipate in return when your surrender is coupled with a right-hearted spirit?

SECTION 3: *Personal Time*

She shall be called Woman, because she was taken out of Man.
GENESIS 2:23

One of the most frequent comments I hear in marital counseling is this complaint from a couple that isn't getting along: "We are not compatible. We are as different as night and day."

In light of God's design for marriage, this is one of the most uninformed statements a husband or wife can make. Of course the two people are different! God planned them to be different. The reason a husband and wife need each other is because they *are* different. While you are dating and in the engagement stage, your differences may not show up as boldly as they will when you are married. It's easy to overlook things when you are first in love. But trust me, the two of you are different. You just may not realize how different until you've been married awhile.

One of the sweetest blessings God has given me is a woman who has a personality totally different from mine. I'm an outgoing, very public person-ality while my wife, Lois, is poised, deliberate, and orderly. Because we have contrasting personalities, when I'm too outgoing, her reserve pulls me back. And when she is too reserved, my enthusiasm pulls her forward.

Yes, this does occasionally cause friction between us, but those are minor distractions to our overarching goals as a married couple. Our primary goal remains to make our God-given differences work for us instead of against us, to be enhanced by our differences, both personally and in the ministry.

When God brought Eve to Adam, he recognized immediately how dis-tinctly different she was from him—and he was excited about those differ-ences. Adam also knew that Eve was part of him; she made him complete. Adam called Eve "bone of my bones, and flesh of my flesh" (Genesis 2:23). Theirs was truly a match made in heaven! Now, it's true that the presence of sin has clouded this understanding of the oneness and unity of the marriage partnership. However, if you would look for what God is trying to teach you through the mate He has given you, you would do more growing through your relationship than griping about it.

Your differences also enable you to fulfill and carry out the divinely designed roles God has for you to satisfy in your marriage. As with everything God has created, there is an order to it that, when followed, allows things to run smoothly. Order has nothing to do with equality or value. Both partners in a marriage are of equal value. Order has everything to do with . . . well, order. You and I both appreciate the fact that we have order on our roads and highways, right? I know I do. Order provides the opportunity for forward progress and enjoyment to occur. Without it, life (and marriages) can end up in a heap of a mess.

Reflect & Respond

Spend a few moments discussing with your fiancé the answers to the following questions based on this week's devotional thought.

1. Identify some ways that you and your fiancé are not alike. It may be a challenge to look for differences at this stage in your relationship, but dig deep and you'll find some.

2. Discuss ways that your differences can wind up being an asset to your relationship rather than a hindrance. Come up with one practical example where you have already experienced how your differences brought about a positive result.

3. Think of examples of people you know (they could be family members or friends) whose differences complement each other. Share what you have observed about them and also what you would like to apply in your own marriage relationship.

4. The Father, Son, and Holy Spirit are equal in value and one in essence (John 10:30; 15:26), but according to Luke 22:42 and Hebrews 10:7, what did Jesus do with regard to the Father? How can a person submit to someone else but still be of the same value?

5. Our salvation is based upon all three members of the Trinity. They carry out different roles even though they are one in nature.

    a. Read John 3:16 and John 10:29. What is the role of the Father in our salvation?

    b. Read 1 John 2:2 and Ephesians 2:6. What is the role of the Son in our salvation?

    c.   Read Ephesians 4:30 and Titus 3:5. What is the role of the Spirit in our salvation?

SECTION 4: *Take-It-In Time*

Mentor Moment

Thriving couples have a deep, shared faith. They consciously regard Christ as the foundation of their relationship (Ephesians 2:20) and understand that a genuinely *Christ-centered* marriage is a marriage in which both partners actively acknowledge the presence and the authority of God, and where Jesus makes an observable difference in daily life.

1.   What do you think it means to have a Christ-centered marriage?

2.   Would you say that your relationship is solidly grounded on the foundation of your faith in Jesus Christ? Why or why not?

3.   What are some practical ways you can acknowledge God's authority in your home? How does the belief that He is present shape your interactions with one another?

4.   What do you do differently as a couple because of your Christian faith? Do you pray together as a couple? Study the Bible? Meet with other believers? Do you think that activities of this kind have an important impact on the quality of your relationship?

5. Have you shared with your fiancé how you came to know the Lord? Do you regularly talk with each other about the things you are learning on your spiritual journey?

6. What does the term "walking with Christ" mean to each of you? How do you differ from one another in the way you approach your faith? In what ways are you similar?

SECTION 5: *Time Together*

Date Night Discussion

Summary Statements: Set aside time to explore the following summary statements in the context of a date or while sharing a meal. Open your discussion time in prayer, asking the Lord to draw you both together in alignment under Him. Begin by reading these foundational principles aloud to each other. Afterward, discuss what they mean to you personally and how you want them to be displayed in your marriage. Finally, discuss the Talking Topics that follow the foundational principles.

- Order is critical because order reveals a heart of obedience and trust. Disorder embodies rebellion and pride.

- All hell broke loose in the garden because Adam and Eve got out of order.

- Had Jesus felt like His rights were being infringed upon as He prayed in the garden of Gethsemane, or that His goals were being impeded and He thus rebelled, we would all be in a world of hurt right now.

Talking Topics: Take time to discuss your histories (childhood, family, education) and how they have shaped your mind-set on roles in relationships. Spend some of the discussion focusing on the good things you observed as well as what you want to be reflected in your own marriage relationship. Share what areas may prove to be more difficult for you to adjust to, and ask your fiancé to pray with you that God will soften your heart, open your mind, and align your thinking, beliefs, and actions under the truth of His Word.

LESSON 3

✤✤✤✤✤✤

OPPOSITION

SECTION 1: *Time with Tony Video Segment*

Begin your time together by opening in prayer, then watch the lesson 3 video segment. (See page ix for link.)

SECTION 2: *Study Time*

Heart Highlights

Read chapter 3 of *Kingdom Marriage* individually. Rewrite the following highlights from the chapter in your own words, or, if you prefer, simply reword the statements in a conversation you have with your fiancé at a later time. Make sure to write them or speak them in such a way that they will personally apply to you and your future spouse.

1. Get this one thing right and all the other things will fall into place: Get a divine perspective on your marriage as the foundation for your home, and you'll discover who your true enemy is—and it is not each other.

2. If you are unable to truly comprehend and correct your focus by making a spiritual connection in everything that goes on in your marriage, you will continue to rant and rave about the fruit, or whatever the current issue is.

3. Satan wants to destroy your marriage not just because he wants to destroy your marriage. He wants to destroy your marriage because he knows that in doing so, he also destroys your legacy. He messes up the future of your children and their children.

4. The primary reason Satan stirs up conflict in our marital relationships is because he wants to flip the rulership in our lives. He is seeking to dethrone the one true King who reigns over both partners in a marriage. Then he wants to offer each partner the misguided notion that they have the wisdom and the ability to live apart from God.

5. When you view your enemy as your spouse and fail to recognize the true enemy, Satan, you are getting hoodwinked. Satan is playing the end against the middle in order to keep both of you from carrying out all God desires to do in and through you.

Digging Deeper

1. Come up with some creative ways you will remind yourself that your partner is not your enemy when conflict arises, ways that will shift your focus to the spiritual warfare behind the issue at hand.

2. How did you witness conflict-resolution in your home growing up or in the relationships of others you've known? Share some of the positives (and negatives) that you would like to keep (or avoid) in your marriage relationship, and why.

3. Satan has been studying each of us for a long time and knows our particular trigger points that create quick agitation. Awareness is often half the battle. List some of the "triggers" that can deflate you quickly in a conflict, and talk about ways to stay aware of these with each other.

4. In what ways does conflict in a marriage relationship prevent the couple from fully manifesting the visible demonstration of the comprehensive rule of God in their lives?

5. Why is it critical for couples to recognize the root of the conflict rather than get caught up in the specific issues at hand? Can you think of an issue you may have had with your fiancé that really wasn't about the issue but was about something deeper? What did you learn from that experience?

Section 3: *Personal Time*

Consider it all joy, my brethren, when you encounter various trials, knowing that the testing of your faith produces endurance.
JAMES 1:2-3

I always used to enjoy a good game of basketball. When I played alone, I was completely unstoppable. When there was no opposition, I could make any play and hit any shot. But some years ago, I had an opportunity to go one-on-one with a star member of the Dallas Mavericks basketball team. Suddenly I wasn't playing so well after all.

My basketball ability wasn't tested when I played without opposition. The test was in how good I was when I went up to shoot and found six-and-a-half-feet worth of opposition staring me in the face.

But that's the way the game of basketball is designed to be played. Having to face strong opposition and learn how to cooperate with teammates to overcome that opposition should make anyone a better player, not a worse one.

That's the way it is with marriage. Life's trials are used by God for our development. It's in learning how to face and overcome opposition and tough times together that you and your future mate will grow closer to each other and to God. Until you face opposition as a couple, you will never really know how strong your marriage is. Learn to view conflict from this vantage point, and you will be halfway to your victory already.

Sure, the enemy will take aim at your marriage. Did you ever notice that Satan didn't bother Adam before Eve was created? As long as Adam was single, Satan left him alone. But as soon as Adam was united with Eve, the attack was launched. Why? Because Satan's long-term goal is to destroy the family, not just the individual. That's why his attacks are focused on the husband-wife relationship, because by destroying that he can get the family as well.

But God has a wonderful way of turning Satan's attacks into faith-building lessons and relationship-strengthening opportunities. If you'll let Him. Again, you must choose to reject the notion that your future spouse is the enemy when conflict comes up, and view the conflict as a tool being used by the real enemy. Resolution will come to those couples who both want it as the ultimate goal. View yourself as a team, partnership, or union whose aim it is to overcome the opposition together. With that viewpoint, you will face conflict from a position of strength.

Reflect & Respond

Spend a few moments discussing with your fiancé the answers to the following questions based on this week's devotional thought.

1. Based on your life experience, what do you think of when you think of married couples and conflict? Describe how you would view a typical marital conflict scene as it takes place. Describe the tones of voice, gestures, language, length, etc. What are some of the positive and healthy aspects of how you view this scene? And what are some of the negative and unhealthy things that show up in your viewpoint of marital conflict?

2. Share about a time in your life when a trial made you stronger. What did you learn from this situation? Discuss how viewing trials as growing opportunities could help shape a healthier view of conflict in marriage.

3. What do you think of when you hear words like "the devil," "demons," or "Satan"? How real is spiritual warfare to you? Another way to ask that is, how seriously do you take it? What are some things you can do to go on the offensive against spiritual attacks?

4. Read Ephesians 6:10-18. In what ways can truth, righteousness, peace, security, God's Word, and prayer guard your relationship as a couple?

5. In what way does nurturing your relationship with Jesus Christ by abiding in Him and His Word strengthen you in the area of spiritual warfare?

SECTION 4: *Take-It-In Time*

Mentor Moment

Couples who go the distance recognize that *spousal conflict is inevitable.* They know that the secret of their success lies in the way they *handle* this conflict, and they embrace the concept that God uses this bumping and jarring to cause them to grow (Proverbs 27:17). They keep short accounts and never let the sun go down on their anger (Ephesians 4:26).

1. Do you welcome conflict or view it as a threat?

2. As a couple, do you have a conscious strategy or game plan for resolving your differences? If not, have you ever stopped to analyze the way you handle conflict? Do you simply get by on knee-jerk reactions?

3. What does it mean to fight fair? Are you comfortable with this concept, or do you tend to feel that any kind of fighting is wrong in marriage?

4. How are you both different? How have your differences shaped and impacted your relationship for better or for worse?

5. Is forgiveness the same as forgetting? Why or why not? Can you forgive and not forget? What does it take for you to move *beyond* conflicts and get on with life?

6. Have you ever had a conflict that eventually led to deeper intimacy and understanding? If so, how did that work?

Section 5: *Time Together*

Date Night Discussion

Summary Statements: Set aside time to explore the following summary statements in the context of a date or while sharing a meal. Open your discussion time in prayer, asking the Lord to draw you both together in alignment under Him. Begin by reading these foundational principles aloud to each other.

Afterward, discuss what they mean to you personally and how you want them to be displayed in your marriage. Finally, discuss the Talking Topics that follow the foundational principles.

- A healthy, vibrant marriage is all about focus. Is your focus on God and His purpose and power? Or is it on you and what you want?

- Whoever owns the family owns the future.

- When you don't see your enemy for who he is—a clever manipulator of deception who knows just the right buttons to push to turn you against each other—you will forever be reacting to your spouse rather than recognizing that he or she is just the vehicle to hinder what God is trying to do.

Talking Topics: Misunderstandings and hurt feelings often arise from blaming or accusing rather than asking for clarification, as well as a failure to seek more information before rushing to judgment. Spend some time asking each other questions about areas or issues you may have been quick to jump to conclusions on. If none come to mind, discuss ways to handle conflict through an intentional effort to slow down, ask questions that clarify the situation, and use words and phrases that don't cast blame on the other person. Also discuss with each other how much "blame" was a part of your upbringing, the damage it may have caused, and why it is important to not carry that sinful habit passed down from Adam into your marriage relationship.

LESSON 4

❖❖❖❖❖❖

OATHS

Section 1: *Time with Tony Video Segment*

Begin your time together by opening in prayer, then watch the lesson 4 video segment. (See page ix for link.)

Section 2: *Study Time*

Heart Highlights

Read chapter 4 of *Kingdom Marriage* individually. Rewrite the following highlights from the chapter in your own words, or, if you prefer, simply reword the statements in a conversation you have with your fiancé at a later time. Make sure to write them or speak them in such a way that they will personally apply to you and your future spouse.

1. A covenant (oath) is a *spiritually binding relationship between God and His people. It is a divinely created bond inclusive of certain agreements, conditions, benefits, responsibilities, and effects.* God's power, provisions, and authority to His people operate under His covenants. Whenever God wanted to formalize His relationship with His people, He would establish a covenant.

2. Another way to understand a covenant is through its synonym, which is *covering*. If and when you operate under God's covenant, you are operating under His covering.

3. In order to fully benefit from God's covering—His power, provisions, authority, peace, and blessing—you not only must be *in* His covenant, but you must align yourself *under* His covenantal rule in your marriage.

4. When two people enter into a covenant, they enter into it along with a third Person, God. Just as the Trinity is made up of three coequal Persons who are one—God the Father, God the Son, and God the Holy Spirit—marriage is an earthly replica of this divine Trinity— the husband, wife, and God.

5. You cannot leave God at the altar and expect to have a thriving relationship. God must join you in your home, according to the characteristics He has set within His covenant. When He does, and when you align yourself within the parameters He has established of love, respect, commitment, and compassion, He can do marvels with your marriage.

Digging Deeper

1. There are three distinctions between a covenant and a contract. Read through these three differences and tell how each ought to impact how marriage is both viewed and approached:

    a. A covenant is more than a business partnership. It involves an intimate relationship. (Deuteronomy 6:4-5)

b. Covenants are designed to bring blessing to the parties involved. (Deuteronomy 29:9, John 10:10)

c. Covenants are ratified with blood. (Exodus 29:16-46, Genesis 15, 17)

2. What is the purpose and benefit of a covering? Describe it in a tangible, physical way, and also in a spiritual way.

3. What are the five characteristics of a spiritual covenant, and how do they play out with regard to the marriage relationship?

4. The covenantal characteristic known as "sanctions" carries with it a cause-and-effect repercussion for choices and actions. Why is it important to keep consequences in mind when making decisions with regard to your family?

5. Both sanctions and inheritance can be passed down through families (for good and for bad). Take some time to ask the Lord to reveal to you any negative things that may have been passed down from your family of origin. Once these have been revealed, pray for removal of these negative consequences and ask God to give you wisdom for how to overcome these particular family-based strongholds.

SECTION 3: *Personal Time*

God created man in His own image, in the image of God He created
him; male and female He created them.
GENESIS 1:27

Why did God create sex? Well, the most obvious reason is for procreation. Another reason, a deeper purpose for sex, is to inaugurate or initiate the covenant of marriage. Whenever God made a covenant, He inaugurated it in blood. The sign of the covenant God made with Abraham was circumcision. All of the males born in Israel were to have the foreskin of their sexual organs removed to signify that they were part of God's covenant people.

Why was circumcision chosen as the sign of the Abrahamic covenant, which established Israel as God's special people and through which Abraham would become the father of many nations? Because this covenant was fulfilled and expanded as Abraham and his male descendants produced children. Therefore, their sexual organs would bear the mark of the covenant as a special sign that they and the children they fathered were set apart to the Lord. The rite of circumcision involved blood, which was part of the covenant.

So it is in marriage. According to Deuteronomy 22:13-15, if a new husband in Israel felt he had reason to suspect his wife was not a virgin when he married her, the woman's parents were to produce the evidence of their daughter's virginity and show it to the elders of the city at the city gate. The evidence was the bloodstained sheet from the bed on which the couple consummated their marriage on the wedding night. If the parents could thus prove their daughter's virginity, she was acquitted, and the husband was fined.

But if there was no blood, meaning the woman was not a virgin before marriage, she could be put to death (see verse 21). Why? Because the marriage covenant was to be inaugurated by blood—and God takes His covenants very seriously.

Reflect & Respond

Spend a few moments discussing with your fiancé the answers to the following questions based on this week's devotional thought.

1. Describe how sexual intimacy serves as a renewal of the covenant, and compare it to the importance of taking Communion as a renewal of spiritual surrender and salvation under Christ.

2. How does your own personal view of physical intimacy align with the spiritual meaning tied to it? In what ways do your views of it need to change in order to align with God's?

3. Seeking forgiveness for previous sexual intimacy prior to marriage is a wise thing to do, if you or your fiancé have been engaged sexually before (either with each other or with someone else). Don't treat this lightly. Spend some time before the Lord in repentance. Be aware of how this may impact your view of each other and be open to discussing it.

4. In what way does a covenant come with more tied to it than a contract?

5. Based on Ecclesiastes 4:9-12, what are the three cords in a marriage relationship? And how does honoring sexual purity impact the strength and closeness of those three cords?

SECTION 4: *Take-It-In Time*

Mentor Moment

Successful relationships are made up of two people who intentionally treasure and honor one another. They do this by *keeping a conscious account* of the things they value about each other. Just as Jesus established the Lord's Supper as a *memorial* of His redeeming work on the cross (Luke 22:19), they commemorate the blessings of their relationship in a *tangible, physical* way—with gifts, celebrations, and meaningful mementos of significant occasions.

1. Why were you attracted to each other in the first place? What do you like and admire most about your future spouse? Make a list and share it with your partner.

2. As a couple, what are some of your most important traditions, rituals, and celebrations? How do you use these traditions to strengthen the tie that binds you to each other?

3. Which of your shared memories are most meaningful to you? What are you doing to keep them alive?

4. Can you honestly say that you regard your partner as a "treasure"? How do you express your feelings of mutual appreciation?

5. How do you respond when romantic feelings ebb and flow? What do you do to fan the flames of romance and keep them burning?

6. How do you talk about each other around other people? In social settings, do you feel valued and appreciated by the other?

SECTION 5: *Time Together*

Date Night Discussion

Summary Statements: Set aside time to explore the following summary statements in the context of a date or while sharing a meal. Open your discussion time in prayer, asking the Lord to draw you both together in alignment under Him. Begin by reading these foundational principles aloud to each other. Afterward, discuss what they mean to you personally and how you want them to be displayed in your marriage. Finally, discuss the Talking Topics that follow the foundational principles.

- Marriage is a supreme covenantal union designed by God to allow both partners to fully maximize their potential in Christ.

- The marriage vows are a serious set of vows that bring with them either blessing or cursing, dependent upon how those vows are honored or dismissed.

- God's power operating in your relationship can do miracles. But His power is best freed to flow when you recognize and respect the marital covenant as a covenant, not merely as a convenient companionship you entered into.

Talking Topics: Take time to discuss how you feel about the differences between a covenant and a contract. Share how you view a covenant as different from a contract, and how that impacts your view of marriage. Describe the importance of alignment in honoring the marriage covenant, placing God as the head (covering) over the couple. How does God get dismissed as head in a marriage relationship? When that happens, what are the steps you should take to return Him to His rightful place?

LESSON 5

❖❖❖❖❖❖

ONENESS

SECTION 1: *Time with Tony Video Segment*

Begin your time together by opening in prayer, then watch the lesson 5 video segment. (See page ix for link.)

SECTION 2: *Study Time*

Heart Highlights

Read chapter 5 of *Kingdom Marriage* individually. Rewrite the following highlights from the chapter in your own words, or, if you prefer, simply reword the statements in a conversation you have with your fiancé at a later time. Make sure to write them or speak them in such a way that they will personally apply to you and your future spouse.

1. When couples focus on remaining two while God is seeking to create oneness in them, then they are inadvertently working against God's purposes.

2. If, according to Jesus (John 17:21), the issue of our unity or oneness is so critical to our witness, what do infighting and divisions say to a watching world about the marriage union, which was established to reflect our Lord?

3. Unity is not uniformity or sameness. Unity is not you being just like your mate. In its simplest form, then, unity is any group of people who are characterized by "oneness," a shared purpose, vision, or direction.

4. We are closest to unity in marriage when we are allowing the Spirit to do His work in us, and pointing to and celebrating that work in each other.

5. A healthy marriage is a unified marriage, where the presence and work of God's Spirit transcends our individual differences.

Digging Deeper

1. Read Matthew 12:25. Explain why this verse is so important to the foundation of a healthy marriage. In what ways can a marriage relationship be "divided" against itself, and what are some steps you as a couple can take to prevent that from occurring?

2. In Ephesians 4:1-6, what are the four things that Paul lists before urging the readers to preserve the unity of the Spirit in the bond of peace, and in what way do these four character qualities help to make preserving unity more attainable?

3. What does the word "unity" mean to you? Compare and contrast that with the definition and explanation given in the chapter.

4. Why is it important to maintain your personal uniqueness when becoming "one" with your marriage partner? List and describe some personal traits and strengths you both have that are different from each other. Explain why you appreciate those traits.

5. Based on James 4:1-2, what is the source of quarrels and arguments between people? How can a spirit of oneness guard against this?

SECTION 3: *Personal Time*

[A husband and wife] are no longer two, but one flesh.
MATTHEW 19:6

When He pronounced the original wedding vows between Adam and Eve, God said that a man must leave his family and join to his wife so that they become one flesh (see Genesis 2:24). This instruction was addressed to men, but of course the leaving and joining in marriage go both ways. The King James Version uses the word "cleave" to describe the joining together of a man and wife. But what does it mean to leave family and cleave to each other?

The word *cleave* itself means to stick to something like glue or to attach oneself in a viselike grip. It's a graphic picture of the union that is to take place between a husband and wife. But cleaving involves much more than a physical coupling of two bodies. It means a totality of union with a whole person. It means embracing oneness of purpose while seeking the well-being of your spouse above your own.

If we are not careful, too often our "Let me love you" words to our spouses actually mean "Let me love me." We men are particularly vulnerable to this error. Our culture teaches men to look to women for their own purposes. So it's easy for a man to bring that mind-set into marriage—where it is devastating. And, of course, wives can become self-centered too. But that's the devil's plan, not God's. Cleaving to your spouse means you have made a total commitment to your partner—not only to his or her body, but also to heart, mind, and soul as well. To love with a spirit of oneness involves compassionately and righteously pursuing what is in the best interest of your spouse.

Soon-to-be-husbands, to cleave to your spouse will mean that you will work hard at pleasing her, not yourself. She needs to know that nothing will ever cause you to pull away from her and tear apart that love relationship. One of a woman's greatest emotional needs is security.

Soon-to-be-wives, cleaving to your spouse includes respecting and supporting him in his efforts to lead the marriage and the family. One of a man's greatest emotional needs is respect.

Yes, cleaving is costly and it requires a commitment, but the reward is an intimacy and oneness that rivals few other blessings you will ever know.

Reflect & Respond

Spend a few moments discussing with your fiancé the answers to the following questions based on this week's devotional thought.

1. As a single, who or what has been your primary go-to for advice, counsel, or even comfort? In what ways will you need to intentionally transition this to your spouse as you seek to leave and cleave in a spirit of oneness?

2. Think about the things your fiancé does or says that bring you the greatest sense of peace, enjoyment, and happiness. Write those things down and then share them with each other to say thank you and to help each other know the actions and types of words that you cherish most.

3. Has there been a time in your experience when you felt like you were doing an act of love for someone else, only to discover later that it was motivated by selfishness? What was the outcome of this, and what did you learn about the nature of selfless love?

4. *Oneness* does not mean *sameness*; rather it means oneness of purpose. List separately the top five purposes you have for your future marriage relationship. Then compare those with your fiancé's list and see how many are aligned. Discuss any differences.

5. Cleaving is not the same thing as controlling. In what way does a shared, intimate oneness free each partner up to have his/her own schedule, activities, and pursuits?

SECTION 4: *Take-It-In Time*

Mentor Moment

A thriving marriage is made up of two thriving individuals. It can only be as strong as its component parts—namely, husband and wife. It's a *blending*, not a *cloning*, of two distinct personalities. Common sense itself suggests that healthy relationships emerge when healthy people come together in a healthy, positive way. This means that there's a place for appropriate self-care and self-improvement in any marital relationship (Galatians 6:4-5).

1. What are the most cherished dreams and goals for each of you? What are you doing to achieve them? Does your fiancé approve or disapprove?

2. Are you both comfortable with the idea of taking time out of your schedules for the express purpose of nurturing and caring for *yourself*? Why or why not?

3. Do each of you have a strong devotional life? What do you think it means to spend time with God? What steps are you taking to help yourself grow as a Christian?

4. Is lifelong learning and education—whether formal or informal—important to you? What interests, hobbies, or activities are you pursuing outside of your marriage, your job, and your life at home? What do you like to do with your spare time?

5. What are you doing to stay physically healthy? Are you exercising, eating right, and getting sufficient sleep?

6. How are you encouraging your partner to pursue personal and spiritual self-development? Is there anything practical you can do to create more space and freedom for your mate?

7. To what extent do you look to your partner to meet your needs, fulfill your expectations, or bring significance and meaning to your life? Do you think this is healthy or unhealthy?

Section 5: *Time Together*

Date Night Discussion

Summary Statements: Set aside time to explore the following summary statements in the context of a date or while sharing a meal. Open your discussion time in prayer, asking the Lord to draw you both together in alignment under Him. Begin by reading these foundational principles aloud to each other. Afterward, discuss what they mean to you personally and how you want them to be displayed in your marriage. Finally, discuss the Talking Topics that follow the foundational principles.

- The principle of unity must be understood and vigorously pursued if a marriage is to truly experience God's manifest presence in its midst.

- The greatest gift you can give your unity is maintaining your individual uniqueness. Because then, when two strong and sure people come together under the Lord, utilizing their gifts, minds, and spirits according to His plan, a greater kingdom impact will occur.

- The success of your mission to glorify God and make Him known is tied to your unity in marriage.

Talking Topics: Take time to discuss your views of oneness, unity, and your joint purpose. Share how your parents' or grandparents' relationships demonstrated healthy models of unity, if they did. Let each other know how important maintaining personal distinctions is to you, if it is, and offer some ways to encourage that.

Discuss the value of honoring each other's personal preferences and some ideas you may have about protecting your own personalities while simultaneously merging a oneness of mission and purpose. Describe examples of marriages where you have seen this work well, as well as some examples where you have seen it not work well.

PART II

The Function of a
KINGDOM MARRIAGE

LESSON 6

✤✤✤✤✤✤

ROLES

Section 1: *Time with Tony Video Segment*

Begin your time together by opening in prayer, then watch the lesson 6 video segment. (See page ix for link.)

Section 2: *Study Time*

Heart Highlights

Read chapter 6 of *Kingdom Marriage* individually. Rewrite the following highlights from the chapter in your own words, or, if you prefer, simply reword the statements in a conversation you have with your fiancé at a later time. Make sure to write them or speak them in such a way that they will personally apply to you and your future spouse.

1. Husbands should not be in the marriage first and foremost to get *their* needs met, but rather first to look out for the interests and needs of their wives. A husband's love should be characterized by sacrifice for the good of his wife.

2. The other three principles are knowing, honoring, and praying with your wife. To live with your wife means to dwell in close harmony with her, making your home a place of intimacy and mutual support.

3. Based on the historical law of first mention with regard to marriage in the Bible, companionship wasn't God's primary concern when He made the woman. It was about empowerment—to exercise rule in His name at an even greater level than alone.

4. When a woman truly learns how to submit and does so biblically as to the Lord, this opens the door for God to operate on her behalf in the life of her husband.

5. Jesus is the best example of this lived out in the flesh. Most of the time, He and God were on the same page. But when they weren't, and He asked God to take the cup from Him, He also ultimately submitted. Jesus *chose* to place Himself under God the Father's authority even though they are both equal and have all the characteristics of divinity.

Digging Deeper

Note: In this lesson, we're going to do things a little differently. I'm going to divide up the questions between the men and women.

MEN
1. Read and memorize Galatians 2:20.

2. In this chapter, I call for a husband to be his wife's savior. What is the key concept behind being your partner's savior?

3. In what specific ways have you modeled the concept of dying to self in your relationship? List a few ways.

4. What challenges or obstacles exist in your relationship that make it difficult for you to carry out your role as a savior and sanctifier?

5. How can these challenges or obstacles be overcome?

6. What can your partner do to assist you as you strive to die to self and overcome selfishness in your relationship?

WOMEN
1. Read and memorize Ephesians 4:2-3.

2. In this chapter, I call for wives to exercise the practice of submission to their husbands. What is the key concept behind submitting to your spouse?

3. Who usually makes most of the major decisions in your relationship? Why do you think that is?

4. Does your partner consider your input when major decisions are being made?

5. What decisions, major or minor, is your fiancé facing at this time that he earnestly needs your encouragement and support with?

6. How can you respect your fiancé more in his role of leadership?

SECTION 3: *Personal Time*

Now the serpent was more crafty than any beast of the field which the LORD God had made.
GENESIS 3:1

It should not surprise us that the first family sin stronghold in history was the work of Satan. He has always sought to infiltrate the family, and his methodology is simple. He got our first parents to reverse their biblical roles and responsibilities, a trick he's still using today. We could summarize what Satan told Eve in Genesis 3:1-5 with two statements: "You don't need God. And you don't need Adam."

Satan convinced Eve to act independently of God. He tempted her to use her own reasoning and her own logic to reverse God's established order. Satan then influenced Adam to become a passive male and stand on the sidelines. And when that happened, Satan had an open door to infiltrate the home.

The result was a staggering curse pronounced by God in Genesis 3:14-19. Now there would be conflict in the home where at first there had been peace. God said to Eve, "Your husband . . . will rule over you" (verse 16).

In other words, men would seek to control women by domination. As evil as it is, as wrong as it is, men would seek to dominate women. And the desire of the woman for relationship and for partnership would become a battle rather than a blessing.

God cursed the ground so that from then on the man would become tired from trying to wrestle a living out of a stubborn earth. So instead of coming home to serve his wife, he would come home expecting to be served by her, and that would produce conflict. And after all this, Adam and Eve had to endure the murder of one son by another.

Obviously, Satan's stronghold in Adam's family was passed on to the next generation. Exodus 20:5 says that can happen. But look at the promise of the very next verse: God says He will "[show] lovingkindness to thousands, to those who love Me and keep My commandments" (verse 6).

Reflect & Respond

Spend a few moments discussing with your fiancé the answers to the following questions based on this week's devotional thought.

1. Read 1 Corinthians 11:11 and Ephesians 5:33.

2. In marriage, alignment in our roles involves aligning our thoughts, our actions, our decisions, and our leadership underneath the overarching viewpoint and authority of God. What tasks would you deem non-negotiable when it comes to *you* completing them in your home? Are there any tasks you believe you should not be asked to do in the home?

3. What areas in your relationship do you feel your partner is struggling to bring into proper alignment? What areas are you struggling to align in the concept of roles?

4. What can each of you do to assist the other to become properly aligned?

5. Living within proper roles (or not) can bring blessings or curses. What blessings or consequences have you experienced in your relationship because you have not adhered to God's rules?

6. Continuity is God's desire to pass the blessings of your relationship to the next generation. What blessings are you experiencing that you hope to see passed to the next generation?

SECTION 4: *Take-It-In Time*

Mentor Moment

Couples with vibrant relationships find ways to resolve the issue of male and female roles between themselves with Scripture as their guide. They talk openly about their expectations and personal preferences and hammer out a God-honoring plan that preserves fairness and equity in the way it divides household tasks and responsibilities. Their goal is to "bear one another's burdens" (Galatians 6:2) and function as a *team*.

1. Are you happy with the way you've divided up future household chores and responsibilities?

2. How did your parents approach the question of male and female roles in marriage? How has the example of the older generation shaped your own attitudes toward this sometimes sensitive aspect of the marital relationship?

3. What is your understanding of what the Bible has to say about the roles of husbands and wives? Is that reflected in your relationship so far?

4. What kind of household tasks do you enjoy most? What are you best at—in other words, where do your personal gifts, interests, and talents lie? How do *you* think you can best serve your spouse?

5. What do you *expect* your spouse to do for you? Wash your clothes? Maintain the car? Cook your dinner? Bring you the newspaper or breakfast in bed? What are your assumptions about your *own* role in the marriage and your *own* contribution to the relationship? Write down your answers to these questions and share them with one another.

6. Have you taken the time to discuss, organize, and codify these expectations and assumptions? Maybe you want to draw up a plan, make a chart detailing each partner's chores, and post it on your refrigerator.

7. When it comes to sharing the load of household chores and responsibilities, are you on the same page, or does it look as if this is going to be a bone of contention in your marriage? If it's a source of conflict, what can you do to smooth the waters?

SECTION 5: *Time Together*

Date Night Discussion

Summary Statements: Set aside time to explore the following summary statements in the context of a date or while sharing a meal. Open your discussion time in prayer, asking the Lord to draw you both together in alignment under Him. Begin by reading these foundational principles aloud to each other. Afterward, discuss what they mean to you personally and how you want them to be displayed in your marriage. Finally, discuss the Talking Topics that follow the foundational principles.

- The family is the fundamental institution in society, so it is crucial that we understand our roles as husbands and wives through God's perspective.

- A kingdom man is *a male who places himself underneath God's rulership and lives his life submitted to the Lordship of Jesus Christ.*

- A kingdom woman is *a woman who positions herself under and operates according to the rule of God over every area of her life.*

Talking Topics: Take time to discuss your viewpoint on men's and women's roles in marriage. Share what you agree with from the reading and video material and what portions you may feel differently about. Be sure to look at places where you need to come together as a couple in alignment. Don't be afraid to discuss disagreements ahead of time about this all-important subject. Iron out your expectations now and it will pay dividends in the future.

LESSON 7

✦✦✦✦✦✦

RESOLUTIONS

SECTION 1: *Time with Tony Video Segment*

Begin your time together by opening with prayer, then watch the lesson 7 video segment. (See page ix for link.)

SECTION 2: *Study Time*

Heart Highlights

Read chapter 7 of *Kingdom Marriage* individually. Rewrite the following highlights from the chapter in your own words, or, if you prefer, simply reword the statements in a conversation you have with your fiancé at a later time. Make sure to write them or speak them in such a way that they will personally apply to you and your future spouse.

1. Although the marriage relationship is one of the most rewarding relationships we can enjoy, it can also be one of the most challenging. No other relationship requires such an intense and ongoing level of mutual exchange, sharing of resources, emotions, communication, patience, passion, and more. Simply by its design, the marriage partnership sets itself up to be one of the most testing, trying, and even exhausting relationships in life.

2. When we make seeking and serving God our highest calling, as it should be, then anything that equips or enables us to do this better ought to be embraced.

3. What we need to remember in situations of conflict is that God always has a purpose for the pain (Romans 8:28) when you commit that pain to Him and His will. Your spouse is not your enemy but rather a tool sometimes allowed by God to soften your edges, strengthen your weak spots, and deepen the authenticity of both your faith and your love.

4. Your fiancé is a gift given to you by God to better enable you to carry out your divine destiny in life, and vice versa. Yet, God can and often does use people in our lives to develop our spiritual maturity and character.

5. Read 2 Corinthians 12:7-10. The first place to start in applying Paul's spiritual principles about thorns to our marriages is to admit that marriages come with thorns simply because both the husband and the wife are human. Marriages come with pain. To ignore that reality, or to dismiss it, will only make the wounds fester and grow rather than accomplish what they were designed to do—keep us from exalting ourselves, display the power of Christ, and help us mature.

Digging Deeper

1. Why do you think the marriage relationship offers so many opportunities for conflict, dissatisfaction, and frustration? How do you anticipate that you and your fiancé will approach these issues once you are married?

2. In what way does having a biblical worldview about disturbances in our lives and marriages help guide your response and reaction when these disturbances happen? What is the main kingdom worldview toward the "thorns" God allows?

3. What are some character qualities (virtues) God desires to produce in us through the process of enduring trials and difficulties? How valuable are these virtues?

4. Is there anything in your engagement that has caused you frustration with your fiancé or your situation? Take this to the Lord in prayer. Ask Him to remove it or change it. Let Him know that if He chooses not to, you want to gain the insight He desires you to have as a result of it. Note: If this is serious, this could be a warning sign from God saying "slow down" or "abandon ship" prior to the marriage.

5. Is seeking and serving God your highest priority? What actions and reactions do you have in your life that would back up that answer if you said yes? If your answer is no, what can you or should you change to make it your highest priority (Matthew 6:33)?

SECTION 3: *Personal Time*

Do not let the sun go down on your anger.
EPHESIANS 4:26

The Bible says that anger unleashed wrongfully is hard to overcome. According to Proverbs 18:19, "A brother offended is harder to be won than a strong city." How many times have you wished you could take back something you said or did?

Some people say, "I just explode, and then it's all over." Well, so does a shotgun. But when the smoke clears, a shotgun blast leaves some serious damage behind! People who know it's wrong to explode may deal with their anger by stuffing it, suppressing it, pretending nothing is wrong, or letting it build up. But the Bible says there is an appropriate way to express and deal with anger when disappointments and thorns show up in your relationship. The key is to learn the proper timing.

Ephesians 4:26 gives us the parameters for when we should do something about our anger, but Paul is not necessarily saying that no matter what happens in a day, we just need to kiss and make up and get over it before we go to bed. Some conflicts simply can't be resolved completely in one day. Paul wasn't necessarily telling us not to go to bed until the problem is fixed.

Instead, don't let the sun go down without addressing the issue. That may involve settling things through prayer and an acknowledgment of what has happened. But if the problem is really serious, obeying the Bible may involve simply agreeing to deal with it the next day. The point is that the issue that caused the anger won't be ignored or swept under the rug. It's on the agenda to address and won't be ignored. One of the best ways to have a spirit of ongoing resolution in your relationship is to never negate or dismiss hurt feelings, even if you don't feel they are justified or understand why they occurred. Always make yourself available to listen, respond, and pray.

Reflect & Respond

Spend a few moments discussing with your fiancé the answers to the following questions based on this week's devotional thought.

1. Based on 2 Corinthians 9:8, what does grace give us the ability to do? Spend some time memorizing this all-important verse and thinking of ways to apply it to your life.

2. What are some appropriate ways of expressing anger or pain in a relationship? What are some inappropriate or damaging ways?

3. Whose responsibility is it to control your reactions to your emotional pain? How can God help you do that?

4. How is "power . . . perfected in weakness"? Have you ever experienced this in your own life? Describe what you learned from that situation.

5. Based on Hebrews 12:8-11, what is one reason God allows difficulties (thorns) in our lives?

6. Forgiveness is paramount, but forgiveness does not mean bearing under neglect and/or adultery. What are some healthy ways to address neglect, abuse, or adultery?

SECTION 4: *Take-It-In Time*

Mentor Moment

Successful couples don't consider it strange when external trials and pressures come upon them (1 Peter 4:12). Instead, they *prepare* for hard times and make provisions for seeking outside help when it's needed. In all kinds of adversity, they take pains to anchor their marriage to the solid rock of faith in Jesus Christ.

1. Where do you turn when trouble comes your way? Do difficulties throw you into turmoil, or do you take them in stride?

2. As a couple, have you ever taken time out to discuss how you expect the pressures of the different *stages* of marriage—for example, childbirth, parenting, the empty nest, physical separations, financial setbacks, retirement, illness, and aging—are likely to impact your relationship? Do you have a plan or strategy to help you cope with such eventualities?

3. Is your house built upon sand or rock? What practical steps can you take together to strengthen the *foundation* of your relationship?

4. We've said that conflict, when handled appropriately, can actually strengthen a relationship. Would you say the same thing about adversity and external pressures—for example, the loss of a job or the death of a close family member? Have you ever experienced what it is like to grow closer to one another as the result of weathering a storm together?

5. Do you have a strong support system—friends, family members, or mentors—to whom you can look for help in difficult situations? List the names of the people you'd feel most comfortable turning to for assistance in times of trial.

SECTION 5: *Time Together*

Date Night Discussion

Summary Statements: Set aside time to explore the following summary statements in the context of a date or while sharing a meal. Open your discussion time in prayer, asking the Lord to draw you both together in alignment under

Him. Begin by reading these foundational principles aloud to each other. Afterward, discuss what they mean to you personally and how you want them to be displayed in your marriage. Finally, discuss the Talking Topics that follow the foundational principles.

- Far too many people spend their time planning a wedding with no plan for a marriage.

- God will often use the things and people closest to us to do the greatest work in our hearts, minds, and souls.

- When you pray that God will help you love your fiancé more completely or that your fiancé will love you more deeply, remember this path that teaches and cultivates love: It includes self-control, perseverance, kindness, and more.

Talking Topics: Take time to discuss your normal mode of reaction and response to things like disappointment, disagreements, or being offended. Do you shut down, lash out, blame others, or run away? Talk about ways to help you both go to God in prayer first and then embrace the weakness that comes from trials, seeking insight for spiritual growth and personal maturity. Share with each other your commitment to seek and serve God as your highest priority, and in what ways you can encourage each other to do the same. Make a commitment to each other and God to develop a new way of dealing with difficult situations.

LESSON 8

✠ ✠ ✠ ✠ ✠ ✠

REQUESTS

SECTION 1: *Time with Tony Video Segment*

Begin your time together by opening in prayer, then watch the lesson 8 video segment. (See page ix for link.)

SECTION 2: *Study Time*

Heart Highlights

Read chapter 8 of *Kingdom Marriage* individually. Rewrite the following highlights from the chapter in your own words, or, if you prefer, simply reword the statements in a conversation you have with your fiancé at a later time. Make sure to write them or speak them in such a way that they will personally apply to you and your future spouse.

1. Paul, in the midst of prison and under the weight of possible execution, tells us to be anxious for nothing. He doesn't say be anxious for almost nothing, or even be anxious for those things that are big but not for those things that are little. Paul tells us clearly to be anxious for *nothing*.

2. God is not a compartmentalized God—He is King, Creator, and ruler over all. Because of this, His worldview and perspective ought to come to bear in all that we do. Praying without ceasing augments an ongoing abiding with Christ, which we have been instructed to do so that our lives might be abundant and our prayers might be answered.

3. Paul uses four words for prayer in Philippians 4:6: prayer, supplication, thanksgiving, and requests. The first word, "prayer," has to do with general communication with God. The second word, "supplication," involves the attitude of appealing to God. The third word, "thanksgiving," expresses our gratitude to God, and the fourth word, "request," has to do with being very specific about what we are asking Him to do. When you follow Paul's outline for prayer, it will decrease your propensity to worry.

4. Too often in our relationships, we will react to each other out of our emotions rather than look to God to see how we should respond. Prayer is often neglected when it should be the GPS that guides us as we look to God and His direction in our lives.

5. Make it a point to begin every single day bathing your relationship in prayer. It doesn't have to be long, but it has to be authentic.

Digging Deeper

1. In your own words, define the four different aspects Paul uses to describe how we should pray: prayer, supplication, thanksgiving, and requests.

2. Based on Psalm 46:10, what does it mean (what does it look like in both actions and emotions) to be still and know that God is God? How should that impact our prayers?

3. Read John 15:5. What is the key to producing good things (bearing fruit) in our lives? In what way does abiding in Christ include prayer?

4. Read Psalm 25:1. In what way is prayer a lifting up of your soul to God?

5. Psalm 86 is a great prayer guide. Read and reflect on the entire psalm. What are some qualities David ascribes to God in this prayer? How does he respond to attacks against him? What does he ask God to do at the end of the prayer? In what way can you incorporate a request for favor in your relationship and with each other into your prayer life?

SECTION 3: *Personal Time*

[Jesus] was telling them a parable to show that at all times they ought to pray and not to lose heart.
LUKE 18:1

One of the lessons Jesus taught repeatedly about prayer is that we need to stay at it—to hang in there when we pray. In Luke 18:1-8, Jesus taught this truth through the parable of an uncaring, unfeeling judge and a widow who was being harassed by someone. Now, even though widows were the most power-less people in Jesus' day, this widow was so persistent in appealing to the judge that she finally wore him down, and he granted her request.

Jesus was saying that if persistent asking can wear down an uncaring judge and make him act on a person's behalf, how much more quickly will our loving, caring God respond to the heartfelt cries of His people?

The original language here helps explain why God is so ready to respond to persistent prayer. The judge in Jesus' story was not worried that this widow was going to punch him in the eye, but that his reputation would be harmed if he didn't help her. We use the same term today when we talk about someone giving us a black eye. We mean that the person has harmed our reputation.

Now, if an unrighteous judge is careful about his reputation, which can't be that good, how much more is the righteous judge of all the earth concerned for His reputation and His glory? So, Jesus says, be persistent in prayer because God will act out of regard for His own glory, as well as His concern for His children.

The point of the parable, then, is that you should persistently exercise your legal right to access heaven's intervention on earth. Notice that Jesus only gave us two options in prayer: praying faithfully or losing heart. When you are tempted to lose heart or become discouraged in prayer, that's your signal that it's time to pray all the harder.

Reflect & Respond

Spend a few moments discussing with your fiancé the answers to the following questions based on this week's devotional thought.

1.   How persistent would you say your prayer life is? In what ways can you become more persistent, and what are some things that could help you in that area?

2.   Have you ever considered including in your prayers how the requested outcome can or will impact the glory of God? God is interested in His own glory; in what ways can you include this aspect more in your prayers?

3.   How often do you pray for your fiancé? Are you satisfied with that amount of time, or can you increase it? What reminder can you put in place to pray more for your fiancé?

4. Has there been a time in your life when you saw things change as a result of your prayers? What did you learn from this?

5. When Paul tells us to "pray without ceasing," that is similar to "persistent prayer." Does God get annoyed by repeated requests, or have we been instructed to keep an ongoing dialogue with Him? Name some ways you can pray without ceasing while going about your daily activities.

SECTION 4: *Take-It-In Time*

Mentor Moment

Communication is the heart and soul of any vibrant relationship. Just as prayer is critical for your relationship with God, healthy communication is critical in your marriage as well. Successful husbands and wives understand this. They prioritize communication and approach it as a *process* involving openness, empathy, and a deep heart connection. They are quick to listen and slow to speak (James 1:19). They ask questions and try to understand each other's thoughts and feelings.

1. How often do you sit down as a couple simply to *talk* to one another? Do you set aside time specifically for this purpose? Why or why not?

2. What do you *need* and *expect* from each other in terms of openness and depth of communication? How do your needs and expectations differ?

3. Do you feel that you understand each other? If not, what can you do to improve the situation?

4. Males and females often have different communication styles. Have you found this true in your relationship? How do you work through the challenges this can bring?

5. If you had three minutes to explain yourself to your partner, what would you say? Is there anything about your partner that you want to understand more clearly?

6. Do you find it easy or difficult to be together for any length of time *without* talking?

7. Has your partner changed significantly since the two of you started dating? How does your current relationship differ from that beginning?

SECTION 5: *Time Together*

Date Night Discussion

Summary Statements: Set aside time to explore the following summary statements in the context of a date or while sharing a meal. Open your discussion time in prayer, asking the Lord to draw you both together in alignment under Him. Begin by reading these foundational principles aloud to each other.

Afterward, discuss what they mean to you personally and how you want them to be displayed in your marriage. Finally, discuss the Talking Topics that follow the foundational principles.

- You cannot change the way you feel until you change the way you think, because what controls the way you think will determine the way you feel.

- Prayer is relational communion with God. It is earthly permission for heavenly intervention, and it is a powerful tool in the hands of anyone.

- Living with each other in a spirit of honor and unity will open the pathway to a more effective prayer life.

Talking Topics: Take time to discuss your background and history regarding prayer. How important has prayer been in your life? In what ways do you wish you could pray more effectively? Why do you think that showing each other a spirit of honor and unity will open the pathway to effective prayer? How does prayer help to align our thoughts underneath God's rule? Discuss a prayer strategy for you as a couple that you can agree on.

LESSON 9

✣ ✣ ✣ ✣ ✣ ✣

RESTORATION

SECTION 1: *Time with Tony Video Segment*

Begin your time together by opening in prayer, then watch the lesson 9 video segment. (See page ix for link.)

SECTION 2: *Study Time*

Heart Highlights

Read chapter 9 of *Kingdom Marriage* individually. Rewrite the following highlights from the chapter in your own words, or, if you prefer, simply reword the statements in a conversation you have with your fiancé at a later time. Make sure to write them or speak them in such a way that they will personally apply to you and your future spouse.

1. Just as the first marriage suffered a breakup due to the root cause of an interfering angel of darkness, every family breakup has as its root cause Satan and his desire to destroy that home. That's why forgiveness is such a critical element of a healthy marriage—because when you or I are living in a state of unforgiveness toward someone else, God says He will not live in a state of relational forgiveness with us (Matthew 6:15).

2. It is often the prolonged buildup of anger that provides the opportunity for Satan to turn a problem in a marriage into a stronghold. If you have allowed anger to accumulate over time and have not chosen to address it or sought help to address it, it will open the door for spiritual warfare to wreak havoc on your home.

3. If you know that whatever you are discussing or doing is going to end up as a potential conflict, then set a specific time in the future when you will be able to discuss it rationally, without the heat of emotion.

4. Unforgiveness is like an untreated wound in the soul. It boils over with the heat of bitterness and sets a cycle in motion where small scuffles become large wars (Hebrews 12:15). When the wounds in our hearts are left untreated, they rot, thus producing residual pain in other areas of our lives.

5. Only when you commit your conflict to prayer, healthy communication, humility, and forgiveness will you experience the power to overcome marriage strongholds.

Digging Deeper

1. In what way has unforgiveness negatively impacted your life, whether it's your own or someone else's you've experienced through a relationship, family situation, or work environment? What lessons can you learn from it about the dangers of unforgiveness?

2. Have you ever overreacted due to an unhealed wound from the past that was not related to your fiancé but was aimed at your fiancé nevertheless? Take some time to think of potential emotional triggers that may be tender, and look for ways to be proactive in healing these areas of bitterness or unforgiveness so they don't spill over into your relationship.

3. What role does humility play in conflict resolution and forgiveness?

4. Are there any areas of anger or unresolved emotional pain between you and your fiancé? List what these are, if any. Pray for wisdom on how to approach them in a manner that will lead to mutual understanding, validation, and forgiveness.

5. How do you feel about the suggestion to set aside one time per week to allow for venting, with the condition that the remainder of the week will not include nagging or complaints? In what way could this improve your relationship? What might be a challenge with this approach?

6. Create a list of your top five negative triggers, then share them with each other.

SECTION 3: *Personal Time*

Keep fervent in your love for one another, because love covers a multitude of sins.
I PETER 4:8

I have a steel plate in my lower right leg, a souvenir from my earlier football days. I had just made an interception from my linebacker spot when I was hit with a cross-body blow. My right leg stayed planted on the ground, and I heard a loud crack. The two bones in my lower leg were shattered. The ambulance came onto the football field and rushed me to the hospital, where a surgeon opened up my leg, put the bones back together, and screwed a steel plate onto the bones to hold them in place. That was in 1970, and the plate has been there ever since.

The ugly scar on my leg is a reminder of the excruciating pain of that injury. My leg had a multitude of broken places, but the surgeon knew exactly what he was doing. He made the right incision at the right place at the right time, and he used the right instruments. The result is that today, my formerly shattered right leg is stronger than my left leg that has never been broken.

Love can do the same thing for people with broken places, people whose lives have been shattered by sin. Now don't misunderstand. We're not talking about covering it up or sweeping it under the rug and pretending it didn't happen. Sin always has to be dealt with. But the idea here is that love does not keep bringing up the other person's sin or constantly reminding the person of his or her sin or refuse to give him or her another chance. Instead, love "bears all things" (1 Corinthians 13:7) by forgiving the sinner as we remember we are forgiven people ourselves.

What better place to practice the healing ministry of love than in your romantic relationship? Every intimate relationship needs forgiveness to survive and thrive. Godly love can put the broken pieces back together and affix a steel plate over the weak area, making it even stronger than it was before.

Reflect & Respond

Spend a few moments discussing with your fiancé the answers to the following questions based on this week's devotional thought.

1. Describe what you think the Scripture means when it says, "love bears all things" and "love covers a multitude of sins."

2. In what way can love bring healing and strength to emotions or hearts that have been broken?

3. What is the best way to respond to someone who is angry and overcome with negative feelings? Discuss ways to short-circuit the fuse and bring a healthy calm into the conversation.

4. Are you willing to let go of past hurts (or future hurts when they are committed) and agree not to bring up reminders of failures in your relationship? Think of something that you can agree on to say or do to remind each other of this decision. It could be a code word, special look, or phrase.

5. How do you think forgiveness can actually make a relationship stronger than it was before? Have you experienced this in your own life? Share what the result was.

Section 4: *Take-It-In Time*

Mentor Moment

In healthy relationships, couples realize that they need to grant forgiveness as much as they receive it. They are intentional about giving the benefit of the doubt when a misunderstanding has occurred. They make it a point to communicate about any hurts, confusion, or wrongdoing in a way that is both respectful and kind. They offer forgiveness after the model of Jesus Christ Himself.

1. Would you say that forgiveness is something you experience freely in your relationship? Or do you see more times than not that conflict leads to a grudge or continued difficulties over time?

2. What are you doing as a couple to cultivate a heart of mutual trust and understanding? In what ways has your experience with forgiveness in the past impacted how freely you are willing to give it today?

3. How would you describe yourself—as "quick to anger" or "quick to forgive"? Why did you choose what you did? How would you describe your partner?

4. Do you have a strategy in place for when an offense has occurred?

5. Have you as a couple ever found yourself in a place where you are not willing to forgive the other person, at least for a time? What happened and how was it resolved?

SECTION 5: *Time Together*

Date Night Discussion

Summary Statements: Set aside time to explore the following summary statements in the context of a date or while sharing a meal. Open your discussion time in prayer, asking the Lord to draw you both together in alignment under Him. Begin by reading these foundational principles aloud to each other. Afterward, discuss what they mean to you personally and how you want them to be displayed in your marriage. Finally, discuss the Talking Topics that follow the foundational principles.

- You have to turn unforgiveness over to God and replace your thoughts of anger, hurt, and pain with those of thanksgiving—thanksgiving that God has given you the faith and ability to be released from the stronghold of unforgiveness.

• Biblical forgiveness is the decision to no longer credit an offense against your spouse with a view of enacting vengeance. It means you release your spouse from a debt owed to you, as well as the blame he or she may deserve due to what they did. Forgiveness is first and foremost a decision. It does not begin with an emotion.

• Healing comes from a place of understanding and validation. When you allow your spouse the freedom to communicate what has pained him or her, and you validate that pain through not defending it or saying he or she is wrong to feel it, you will be amazed at how quickly healing and forgiveness will come.

Talking Topics: Take time to discuss your experience with anger, bitterness, and forgiveness in life. Is there anyone you still need to forgive? Try to resolve these emotions and heal from these hurts rather than bringing them into your upcoming marriage. Pray together and ask the Lord to bring about His miraculous healing power in your hearts. Talk through potential trigger points that may be sensitive so that you will both be aware of ways to honor each other's emotions in what might be delicate areas of discussion.

LESSON 10

❖❖❖❖❖❖

RESOURCES

SECTION 1: *Time with Tony Video Segment*

Begin your time together by opening in prayer, then watch the lesson 10 video segment. (See page ix for link.)

SECTION 2: *Study Time*

Heart Highlights

Read chapter 10 of *Kingdom Marriage* individually. Rewrite the following highlights from the chapter in your own words, or, if you prefer, simply reword the statements in a conversation you have with your fiancé at a later time. Make sure to write them or speak them in such a way that they will personally apply to you and your future spouse.

1. Paul spoke of what contentment truly means, which is to "be contained." It means to have the resources available to you in order to handle whatever it is you are dealing with.

2. Contentment means being at rest, thankful, and grateful for whatever situation you find yourself in. You can always know someone's contentment level by whether he or she is complaining or being grateful. If complaints are controlling a person, then there is no contentment. If gratitude is the dominant presence, then there is contentment.

3. It is for God's will that all things exist, whether that be our time, talents, or treasures. We exist for Him.

4. Pride motivated Satan's claim to God's power and ownership. Pride also motivates our desire to claim ownership over the gifts God has given us rather than act as faithful, responsible, and generous stewards.

5. The Lord expects His faithful stewards to invest His gifts in eternal, kingdom purposes.

Digging Deeper

1. Describe some areas of your life where you have known contentment. How important is it to be content when it comes to the material/ financial aspect of life, and in what way does contentment in financial areas manifest itself through your decisions?

2. Why is complaining an indicator of a lack of contentment? Discuss ways in which you can replace complaining with gratitude through a change in your mind-set.

3. Describe "stewardship" as compared to "ownership" through providing a practical example. How can this example illustrate a kingdom perspective on finances?

4. What is the primary purpose of someone who is stewarding the resources of another?

5. Read Hebrews 12:28 and Job 1:21. What is to be our primary response to all that God gives to us? Name some ways we can regularly and proactively demonstrate this response to the Lord with what He has entrusted to us.

SECTION 3: *Personal Time*

Know well the condition of your flocks, and pay attention to your herds.
PROVERBS 27:23

When the Bible tells us not to go into debt, that does not mean we are never to have any financial obligations. It doesn't mean that we can never borrow money for a house or something we need.

Having bills is not how the Bible defines debt. Instead, debt is the inability to pay the financial obligations we have made. It is being in such financial bondage that we are hampered in our ability to use our resources in a way that honors God and supports His work. Part of being on top of your finances is understanding how easy it is to fall into the debt trap. People usually fall into debt for one or more of four basic reasons:

1. They are unaware of God's principles of finance. They don't know what God has said about money and debt, so they don't know how to put His Word into practice. As a result, they wind up doing what everybody else is doing, and they fall into financial bondage.

2. They have given in to self-indulgence, impulse spending, and a desire to have *more* no matter what the cost. The Bible calls these things greed, which leads to unwise decisions.

3. They have practiced poor planning. It's amazing how many couples I talk to who have no answer when I ask them to tell me about their

financial plan for living within their budget and staying out of debt. And when people don't plan, they plan to fail.

4. They are the victims of a financial catastrophe. This is one area they may not be able to avoid. It is something that is beyond their control.

Are you in debt right now even before you begin your marriage? Identifying the cause of your debt is the first step toward doing something about it. Then, setting up a plan to reduce and eventually eliminate your debt would be wise. One of the greatest ways to do that is by avoiding adding more debt. Over time, you can pay off your debt and allow yourselves the freedom that comes from not being constrained by a mound of bills.

You may find this counterintuitive, but one of the best ways to get out of debt is by giving. Read that sentence again. This is because God rewards a heart that is willing to share. There are three principles to follow as you seek to get out of debt. They are:

1. Give
2. Save
3. Spend

When you operate according to a hierarchy that places the prominent emphasis on giving and saving, thus allowing you to spend a portion of what remains, you will discover financial freedom. My ministry offers a free downloadable e-book that lists thirty things you can do to live in financial victory. Visit go.tonyevans.org/Christian-free-ebook-financial-victory? for this download.

Reflect & Respond

Spend a few moments discussing with your fiancé the answers to the following questions based on this week's devotional thought.

1.   Describe the difference between debt and financial obligations.

2. How do you feel about tithing, and what are your personal convictions regarding practicing both tithing and giving with your finances?

3. Spend time looking at your current debt situation as individuals, and set up a plan for debt reduction if you have any debt.

4. How important to you are the following: (a) savings, (b) rainy-day funds, (c) retirement funds, (d) travel funds, and (e) debt reduction? Compare your answers and look for areas that need further discussion to get in alignment with each other under God.

5. Whose responsibility will be the handling of bills, bank accounts, and payment plans? Discuss the strengths of each person and where you feel most comfortable in sharing roles or handling tasks individually.

6. Create a budget listing your income and outgoing expenses. Also create a list of your current debts (if any) and then total it. Share this together and discuss a plan.

SECTION 4: *Take-It-In Time*

Mentor Moment

The mutual stewardship of life's resources can be one of the most difficult areas to navigate in a marriage relationship. This is especially true if one partner earns more of the income or if both partners marry later in life with established resources in place. Keeping an open mind about how you approach your resources as a couple will be easier when you both choose to align your thoughts on stewardship underneath God's overarching rule.

1. Have you discussed the approach you will take toward your resources once you are married? Did you discover any points of agreement? Any points of contention?

2. What are you doing now as a couple to strengthen your financial viability?

3. How would each of you describe yourself—as a "frugal person" or a "liberal spender"? How would you describe your partner? Discuss whether your descriptions match up with what the other person thinks.

4. Do you have a strategy in place to approach major financial decisions? What is it?

5. In what ways has your past history with handling finances impacted your present view? Share how that impacts your biblical worldview of finances as well.

Section 5: *Time Together*

Date Night Discussion

Summary Statements: Set aside time to explore the following summary statements in the context of a date or while sharing a meal. Open your discussion time in prayer, asking the Lord to draw you both together in alignment under Him. Begin by reading these foundational principles aloud to each other. Afterward, discuss what they mean to you personally and how you want them to be displayed in your marriage. Finally, discuss the Talking Topics that follow the foundational principles.

- God not only gives to us generously from His resources, but He also rewards us when we care for His resources well. However, He will also hold us accountable if we are lazy.

- Debt is not just about money. For you and your spouse to fully maximize all that God has created you to do to live out your shared purpose as a kingdom couple, you need to get a handle on your resources.

- There is nothing wrong with spending money or enjoying blessings in life. It just needs to be done with wisdom and restraint.

Talking Topics: Take time to discuss your views on finances, debt, and spending. Who were you raised to believe should handle the money in the family? Do you feel that you should have separate bank accounts or a shared account? Why do you feel that way? How important is staying out of debt to you, and what are you willing to give up in order to do so? What do you consider to be "luxuries" in life and what are considered as "needs"? Everyone's definition of both are different, so try to understand what your fiancé thinks about these things.

LESSON 11

✤✤✤✤✤✤

ROMANCE

SECTION 1: *Time with Tony Video Segment*

Begin your time together by opening in prayer, then watch the lesson 11 video segment. (See page ix for link.)

SECTION 2: *Study Time*

Heart Highlights

Read chapter 11 of *Kingdom Marriage* individually. Rewrite the following highlights from the chapter in your own words, or, if you prefer, simply reword the statements in a conversation you have with your fiancé at a later time. Make sure to write them or speak them in such a way that they will personally apply to you and your future spouse.

1. Scientists have researched the effects of kissing along with the transmission of sensory data taking place, ranking a kiss as one of the most profound things a person can do. The impact of a kiss, when all things line up right, can even leave a more powerful sensory imprint on our brains than something as major as the first time a person ever had sex.

2. Romance is such a powerful part of who we are, because God has created us in such a way that we attach to our romantic partner based on our senses, not only on our thoughts, interactions, and conversations with each other.

3. "Kissing can keep love alive when a relationship has survived decades, long after novelty has waned. In other words, kissing influences the uptake of hormones and neurotransmitters beyond our conscious control, and these signals play a huge part in how we feel about each other," reports the *Washington Post*. "A bad kiss, alternatively, can lead to chemical chaos. An uncomfortable environment or a poor match can stimulate the 'stress hormone' cortisol, discouraging both partners from continuing."[1]

4. Through a romantic bond with each other, you find the most authentic form of love possible.

5. Married couples can have sex during their entire marriage and yet never experience *yada*. This is because *yada* involves much more than an action. It includes the romantic attachment, desire, cultivation, and commitment to another person that brings about depth of knowing in a marriage. This is the kind of intimacy that arouses feelings of satisfaction, contentment, happiness, and joy with each other on an ongoing basis.

Digging Deeper

1. Why do you think a kiss can have such an impact on a person's emotions and memories? In what ways does this cause you to want to cherish this aspect of your future married relationship on a higher level than you may have thought before?

2. Describe the difference between romance and physical affection, and also describe how they can cross over and become the same thing.

3. What are the top three romantic things you enjoy about your fiancé? It could be something as simple as he/she knows your favorite drink at Starbucks and orders it without asking. Be sure to share how you feel about these things with him/her.

4. What is your understanding of *yada*, and in what ways can you pursue it with each other?

5. How important is romance to you? How do you define romance? Share your answers with your fiancé.

SECTION 3: *Personal Time*

Eat, friends; drink and imbibe deeply, O lovers.
SONG OF SOLOMON 5:1

Meeting needs and nourishing intimacy in your upcoming marriage is a two-way street. If a husband is meeting his wife's needs, her heart will want to reciprocate, to respond. She does this by coming under her husband's influence. This is what the word *authority* means in 1 Corinthians 7:3-4, where Paul describes the duties of wives and husbands in their physical relationship. *Duty* may seem like a harsh term to apply to a marital sexual relationship; it can be translated today as *willingness* or *offering*.

It is when one spouse willingly releases his or her body to the touch, the care, the caress, and the love of the other, even when the emotions or desire to do so may not be immediately present. When spouses are intimate, there is a giving of themselves, a vulnerability, a yielding of control. When you marry, sexual relations should be the ultimate act of selfless giving rather than a selfish act done to fulfill one's own needs. You can practice this mind-set while engaged by placing the well-being of your fiancé ahead of your own in other areas, such as service or even the direction of conversations.

The Song of Solomon contains the Bible's most unblushing description of sexual intimacy in marriage. Chapter 4 describes the buildup to intimacy in great detail, and the beauty of it is that you see the self-giving between Solomon and his wife, the mutual yielding of their bodies.

When you read that chapter, you'll notice that the intimacy begins with Solomon's compliments, words of admiration, and appreciation for his bride, not with the physical act of sex. But when the moment of intimacy occurs, God Himself issues the invitation of the verse quoted earlier, an invitation to the lovers to enjoy one another.

Satisfying marital intimacy is a matter of meeting each other's needs and of yielding control of your body to your mate. Rather than stifling freedom and spontaneity, such a commitment allows for the full expression of each person's whole self. It is saying, "All of me belongs to all of you."

Reflect & Respond

Spend a few moments discussing with your fiancé the answers to the following questions based on this week's devotional thought.

1. In what way do you view physical intimacy as a releasing of control over your own body and an offering of it to your spouse?

2. Based on chapter 11 of *Kingdom Marriage*, describe the difference between *shakab* and *yada*. Why is it important that physical intimacy involve more than just the act itself?

3. How important is physical appearance to you? Meaning, do you prefer that your fiancé take the time and effort to be intentional in dressing nice and smelling good? Or do you prefer a more laid-back, relaxed look in your partner?

4. What is the most private thing you are willing to share with your fiancé that you may not have yet been willing to share? Take the time to listen to him or her as well. Be sure to guard this trust appropriately.

5. What do you find to be more romantic—kind words, acts of service, touch, or time? Write down the reasons why you chose what you did and how it makes you feel.

6. List your sexual strongholds and any sexual abuse you may have experienced. If you did experience sexual abuse, I strongly recommend that you seek professional counseling so that it does not carry over into your marriage.

SECTION 4: *Take-It-In Time*

Mentor Moment

Thriving couples regularly celebrate their marriages with passionate sexual intimacy. They don't regard sex as a chore or obligation, but as a delightful "dance" in which each spouse puts the other's needs and interests ahead of his or her own (Philippians 2:4). At the same time, they never lose sight of the fact that sex is not the *only* element of a vibrant marital relationship. They understand that satisfying physical intimacy also includes plenty of affection, tenderness, warmth, and physical touch as well.

Note to mentors: Some couples will feel comfortable sharing freely about this topic, others will not. We suggest checking with your mentee couple at the outset to determine whether it would be an appropriate subject for discussion. If they prefer to skip this one, simply move on to the next topic.

1. Do you regularly talk with one another about the physical aspect of your relationship?

2. Are you both mostly "on the same page" when it comes to your views on sexual intimacy, or is this a point of tension or conflict?

3. How do you express affection for one another *outside* of actual sexual intimacy, since you are not yet married? Are you both comfortable and happy with this aspect of your relationship?

4. What are your individual *assumptions* and *expectations* with regard to the sexual side of marriage? How do they compare with your fiancé's? If you differ, what are you doing to resolve the issue(s)?

5. What would you say are the five most important elements of a marriage relationship? If you had to rank these elements, where on the list would you place sex? Can you explain the reasoning behind your ranking?

SECTION 5: *Time Together*

Date Night Discussion

Summary Statements: Set aside time to explore the following summary statements in the context of a date or while sharing a meal. Open your discussion time in prayer, asking the Lord to draw you both together in alignment under Him. Begin by reading these foundational principles aloud to each other. Afterward, discuss what they mean to you personally and how you want them to be displayed in your marriage. Finally, discuss the Talking Topics that follow the foundational principles.

- Within marriage, the chemical bonds of romance that God has given us serve a greater purpose of creating ties of commitment, attraction, and protection.

- Protect each other's hearts and you will be rewarded with deeper intimacy of both body and mind.

- Romance includes bringing joy to each other through a variety of ways, one of which is to always keep your tone, words, and touch imbued with respect as well as allure.

Talking Topics: Take time to discuss the importance of romance to you personally. Be sure to listen to your partner's views on the same subject. Talk about ways that you can make each other feel romantically engaged. Talk through the various questions in this week's lesson and how you felt about the reading material. Although much of the material has to do with your relationship after you are married, take the time to discuss expectations for yourself and each other in the area of sexual intimacy, once married. Respectfully work through any differences that may come up.

LESSON 12

❖❖❖❖❖❖

REBUILDING

SECTION 1: *Time with Tony Video Segment*

Begin your time together by opening in prayer, then watch the lesson 12 video segment. (See page ix for link.)

SECTION 2: *Study Time*

Heart Highlights

Read chapter 12 of *Kingdom Marriage* individually. Rewrite the following highlights from the chapter in your own words, or, if you prefer, simply reword the statements in a conversation you have with your fiancé at a later time. Make sure to write them or speak them in such a way that they will personally apply to you and your future spouse.

1. Rather than tearing down, the Bible instructs us to intentionally build up, develop, and edify each other through what we say.

2. How about rather than pointing out your partner's mistakes to the Lord in prayer (He already knows anyhow), you take the time to thank God for his/her good qualities. Make this a habit and soon you'll experience a shift in your mind-set in how you view and talk to each other.

3. Aren't you glad that God doesn't wait until you deserve His grace in order to give it? Neither should you hold your fiancé hostage to a certain standard in order for you to minister grace to him/her in what you say.

4. How you say it is often just as important as what you say.

5. Intentionally choose tones and language that edify the other person and you will be amazed at what that does to improve your relationship. If you as a couple adopt the attitude and approach of seeking to minister to each other with your words, with the goal of building up one another, you will get less "reaction" from each other and experience less conflict with each other.

Digging Deeper

1. What are five things you cherish about your fiancé? Rather than just name them, go deeper and tell why they mean so much to you.

2. In what way can tone of voice and nonverbal communication increase the impact of what you say when seeking to edify your fiancé?

3. Based on Ephesians 4:29, what is to be the purpose of your words?

4. What is the corresponding theme that appears in the following verses:
   a. Romans 14:19

   b. 1 Corinthians 14:26

   c. Ephesians 4:15-16

   d. 1 Thessalonians 5:11

5. Based on Psalm 19:14, how often should you complain in your conversations with your fiancé or about your fiancé?

SECTION 3: *Personal Time*

Let your speech always be with grace, as though seasoned with salt,
so that you will know how you should respond to each person.
COLOSSIANS 4:6

Here's a resolution for you to make today as a couple: Resolve that you won't waste your disagreements. What I mean by that is, agree together that you won't allow your arguments to simply deteriorate into hurtful words or accusations or name-calling. Promise each other that you won't argue unless each side presents at least one possible solution to the problem.

You may be thinking, "That's a lot of work. I'd just rather get what I have to say off my chest." It may be a lot of work to bend over backward in an attempt to communicate fairly and avoid hurting your fiancé. But one thing is certain: When you bend over backward, you never have to worry about falling on your face.

Yes, it takes work to disagree agreeably with each other. But consider the possible alternatives: screaming and hollering, angry words and thoughts, put-downs, or frosty silences. These things don't have to happen if you follow God's rules for your speech, rules such as "Let no unwholesome word proceed from your mouth" and "Let all bitterness and wrath and anger . . . be put away from you" (Ephesians 4:29, 31).

Instead, the Bible advises us to season our words with salt. Salt is a preservative that keeps rot from setting in. If you'll salt down your words before you say them, you'll preserve your relationship and avoid the kind of words that can spoil a love relationship. Rather, intentionally choose words that are going to build up your relationship. Whether it be in text messages you send reminding each other of what you value or esteem in them, or whether it is a spoken word offered willingly and freely, you can create growth in your relationship by choosing your words wisely.

Season what you say, just like you would want your food seasoned well. Let your words bring delight to each other and watch how that helps you to grow closer and stronger together.

Reflect & Respond

Spend a few moments discussing with your fiancé the answers to the following questions based on this week's devotional thought.

1.   Based on Colossians 4:6, in what way does grace inform what you choose to say?

2. Have you ever considered your words as a ministry? How can you intentionally use what you say to bring about good in your fiancé's life, even when you are having a disagreement?

3. Has anyone ever impacted your life in a major way through something he or she said to you? Take some time to think about how words can shape decisions, worldviews, and even self-perception.

4. In Ephesians 4:29 and 31, what are we instructed to do with bitterness and wrath and anger so that no unwholesome words come out of our mouth? What practical steps can you take to achieve this?

5. Take a moment to think about the most impactful thing your fiancé has ever said to you. Describe why it mattered so much to you and what, if any, positive changes were brought about because of it.

6. For one week, practice overlooking the negative things in your potential partner and highlighting only the positive.

SECTION 4: *Take-It-In Time*

Mentor Moment

Nourishing is a matter of discovering your partner's "love language" and learning how to speak it in words and actions. It's about building each other up in active, practical ways to "encourage one another daily" (Hebrews 3:13). It involves nurturing your partner's strengths and supplementing his or her weaknesses. This implies a significant investment of time and energy, but it's an investment that pays off in a relationship capable of weathering any storm.

1. What energizes and encourages you? Take some time to think about it. Then write down your answers and go over them together.

2. Do you think you have a good understanding of your partner's strengths, weaknesses, desires, and aspirations? If not, what can you do to find out more about these aspects of his or her character and personality?

3. Is there anything you can do to help your partner achieve his or her goals and become the person God wants him or her to be?

4. When you really want to communicate to your partner, "I love you," what do you say or do? What expressions of love do *you* find most meaningful?

5. What are your greatest strengths? Your flaws and weaknesses? List them and share them with your partner. Then talk about ways you can help highlight one another's strong points, complement one another's weaknesses, and help each other become the people God has designed you to be.

Section 5: *Time Together*

Date Night Discussion

Summary Statements: Set aside time to explore the following summary statements in the context of a date or while sharing a meal. Open your discussion time in prayer, asking the Lord to draw you both together in alignment under Him. Begin by reading these foundational principles aloud to each other. Afterward, discuss what they mean to you personally and how you want them to be displayed in your marriage. Finally, discuss the Talking Topics that follow the foundational principles.

- A healthy engagement is one where both partners treat this critical aspect of what they say to one another with care. Your tongue, and what you say, has the ability to steer your relationship toward mutual satisfaction and benefit—or toward mutual despair and harm.

- Your romantic relationship should be that one place where you are encouraged, reminded of your strengths, and given the motivation you need to live out those strengths well.

- The reality is that words do matter, and what you hear affects how you think, feel, and ultimately even how you act. Your mouth reveals your heart and simultaneously affects someone else's heart, for good or for bad.

Talking Topics: Take time to share what you think your fiancé's strengths, gifts, and skills are. Listen to how he/she responds to your words. Does he or she try to deflect compliments? If so, you may need to invest more time in making this a normative part of your conversations. Some people were not raised in an environment where words were used to build each other up. Practice the art of edification and make it a regular routine of your lives together.

LESSON 13

❖❖❖❖❖❖

RETURN

SECTION 1: *Time with Tony Video Segment*

Begin your time together by opening in prayer, then watch the lesson 13 video segment. (See page ix for link.)

SECTION 2: *Study Time*

Heart Highlights

Read chapter 13 of *Kingdom Marriage* individually. Rewrite the following highlights from the chapter in your own words, or, if you prefer, simply reword the statements in a conversation you have with your fiancé at a later time. Make sure to write them or speak them in such a way that they will personally apply to you and your future spouse.

1. Believers can go days or even weeks without having any meaningful communication with the Lord. Or oftentimes the communication we do have is entirely one-sided.

2. First love is different from love. First love always includes something that general *agape* love may not, which is passion.

3. When you feel pain, bitterness, or even simple apathy, quickly focus your thoughts to remembering the feelings of first love. Do this enough times and it will become a habit.

4. Rather than remaining stuck in the muck that piles up over time, consider letting that go and focusing your energy on doing, thinking, and feeling the things you once did, thought, and felt at the start. Seek to re-win, re-woo, re-date, and re-fall in love.

5. We are to remember, repent, and return. Revelation 2:5 says, "Repent and do the deeds you did at first."

Digging Deeper

1. Read Revelation 2:2-4. Describe the difference between doing something out of duty and doing something motivated by a heart of love. Why does the heart motivation matter to Jesus? In what way does it matter to you?

2. Describe some of the actions and words that come about as a result of the passion and fire of "first love."

3. What is one way to rekindle a heart of "first love" when it has become dormant?

4. Have you ever witnessed a relationship that appeared to be over instead be rejuvenated or revived? Share what that was like and how the relationship was restored, as best as you know.

5. Why is it important to keep the flame of "first love" alive, not only in our spiritual relationship with Jesus Christ but in our relationship with our romantic partner? What can happen when it is not kept alive?

Section 3: *Personal Time*

Therefore remember from where you have fallen, and repent and do the deeds you did at first.
REVELATION 2:5

Couples sometimes ask me if a lackluster relationship can be revived. The answer is a resounding *yes*! As long as both of you are still breathing, there is real hope. The formula for restoring a relationship is the same formula Jesus Christ gave to the church for restoring the passion of its initial love for Him.

That formula came in Christ's words to the church at Ephesus, which had been reduced to loveless rituals. Christ offered the members a way to revive their first love: remember, repent, and return. The same principles can revive a couple's relationship.

First, a couple needs to *remember*—to reflect on the early days of their relationship when each season of love was sweet and when love ruled their lives.

If you remember how your relationship was, you'll know it can be that way again. Try to create memories and things that you can look to after you've been married a while to remind you how you felt about each other when you were dating.

Second, the plan calls for *repentance*. To confess that you are wrong is tough, especially when words are not enough. To repent means to change direction. In this case, the right direction is probably toward the early stage of your relationship, when your hearts for one another took precedence over your careers, your friends, and even your own interests.

Finally, a couple needs to *return* to the "deeds" they did at first. That means recapturing something of that earlier relationship. You can't return to the past, but you can bring the works of the past into the present and the future simply by redoing them in a consistent, loving fashion.

Reflect & Respond

Spend a few moments discussing with your fiancé the answers to the following questions based on this week's devotional thought.

1. What is the formula that Jesus gave to His church in order to return to their first love with Him?

2. What reminders can you create during this early phase of your relationship to reflect on when the routine of everyday life sets in after the wedding is over? Maybe it's a photo book or a notepad with your favorite sayings from each other. Get creative in making these reminders of the flame of your first love.

3. What is it about your fiancé that attracted you to him or her? Why did he or she stand out above all others?

4. In what way does our spiritual relationship with God carry over into our love for others? How is returning to your first love with Christ connected to your relationship with each other?

5. Reminisce on the first time you "knew" you were attracted to your fiancé. How did you know, what did it feel like, and how did you respond to your feelings? Be sure to share these answers with each other.

SECTION 4: *Take-It-In Time*

Mentor Moment

Thriving couples are *intentional* about spending enjoyable time together (Philippians 1:8). They build their relationship upon a foundation of shared values, interests, and goals. They schedule regular date nights and outings and develop meaningful traditions and family rituals. They also know how to maintain a healthy balance between togetherness and independence.

1. Do you ever feel that you're simply *too busy* to share enjoyable and meaningful time together? If so, are you satisfied with the status quo, or are you motivated to "fight back"?

2. Is your partner fun to be with? Are *you*? What can you do to foster more spontaneity and laughter in your relationship?

3. What would it take to enable you to spend enjoyable time together on a more regular basis?

4. What *one thing* can you commit yourself to do this week in an effort to free up more time to spend with your partner?

5. Do you have regular date nights? If so, what can you do to keep them from becoming routine and boring? If not, why not?

6. What are your most passionate interests as individuals? What do you enjoy doing most? How would your partner answer these questions? How can you use this knowledge to plan more meaningful times together?

SECTION 5: *Time Together*

Date Night Discussion

Summary Statements: Set aside time to explore the following summary statements in the context of a date or while sharing a meal. Open your discussion time in prayer, asking the Lord to draw you both together in alignment under Him. Begin by reading these foundational principles aloud to each other. Afterward, discuss what they mean to you personally and how you want them to be displayed in your marriage. Finally, discuss the Talking Topics that follow the foundational principles.

- The marriage relationship is one of the most intimate, rewarding experiences in life if you treat it with the honor, attention, and love it deserves.

- The pathway to rekindling your passion of first love is to remember from where you once came.

- What you do doesn't always reveal your heart behind it, but those closest to you—God, your fiancé—know your heart, regardless of what is done.

Talking Topics: This chapter may not have as much relevance to you before you are married. You might want to revisit it after you have been married for a while. But the principles it contains can be used to put some guards in place to help keep your first love in place while you transition into the daily demands of life after the wedding. Take some time to discuss the importance of keeping your heart's affections warm toward each other, even in the midst of busyness and planning. This is important to talk through, especially related to planning the wedding itself. It's easy to get lost in the details so much that you forget to enjoy the reason for doing it in the first place. Discuss possible ways to gently and respectfully remind each other to keep your love alive and fresh. And talk about how important it is that the power and passion of "first love" stay strong between you, when the demands and responsibilities of life start to pile on.

APPENDIX A

✤✤✤✤✤✤

PURPOSE AND PERSONALITIES

WHEN A COMPANY or entity develops a communications and impact campaign around their product or who they are, they come up with several key components such as:

Logo
Tagline
Vision statement

Spend some time drawing or creating your own personal logo on a computer or on paper. Make sure it reflects who you are as a person—strong, quiet, solid, dreamy, etc. Start with your personal logos. Then work with your fiancé to create a couple's logo.

After your logos have been created, develop a tagline for yourselves as a couple that lets others know who you are together in a simple yet creative statement.

Sample Taglines

- **Nike:** Just Do It!
- **Apple:** Think different
- **McDonald's:** I'm Lovin' It
- **Dairy farmers:** Got Milk?
- **M&M's:** Melts in your mouth, not in your hands
- **The Urban Alternative:** Teaching Truth, Transforming Lives

Finally, draft a vision statement that sets the tone and direction for where you want to head together as a couple and what you want to represent to others.

Sample Vision Statements

- **Goodwill:** Every person has the opportunity to achieve his/her fullest potential and participate in and contribute to all aspects of life.

- **Habitat for Humanity:** A world where everyone has a decent place to live.

- **Focus on the Family:** Redeemed families, communities, and societies worldwide through Christ.

- **World Vision:** Our vision for every child, life in all its fullness; our prayer for every heart, the will to make it so.

- **Oceana** seeks to make our oceans as rich, healthy, and abundant as they once were.

- **Make-A-Wish:** Our vision is that people everywhere will share the power of a wish.

- **Teach for America:** One day, all children in this nation will have the opportunity to attain an excellent education.

- **Smithsonian:** Shaping the future by preserving our heritage, discovering new knowledge, and sharing our resources with the world.

Purpose/Identity Quiz

For each statement, circle the letter next to the answer that best reflects the way you think and feel.

1. I am confident that I was created on purpose and for a purpose.

    A. Always   B. Most of the time   C. Sometimes   D. No, I am not sure.

2. I am proud of my name.

    A. Always   B. Most of the time   C. Seldom   D. Never

3. I base the way I feel about myself on my performance at work, at church, or in another activity.

    A. Always   B. Most of the time   C. Seldom   D. Never

4. I tend to feel worthless because I'm not very good at anything.

   A. Always   B. Most of the time   C. Seldom   D. Never

5. My friends and family make it clear that I am important to them.

   A. Always   B. Most of the time   C. Seldom   D. Never

6. I am comfortable being myself around people who are different from me.

   A. Always   B. Most of the time   C. Seldom   D. Never

7. When I want to pick a hairstyle, clothes, or shoes, I get my friends' approval first.

   A. Always

   B. Yes, unless I'm already sure they would approve.

   C. Only if it was something weird.

   D. Why? My friends let me be me

8. I can comfortably discuss my strengths and weaknesses.

   A. Yes, with most people

   B. Yes, with some people

   C. Not really

   D. What strengths and weaknesses?

9. I think most people would reject me if they knew the real me.

   A. Always   B. Most of the time   C. Seldom   D. Never

10. I tend to wonder what will happen to me when I die.

   A. Always   B. Most of the time   C. Seldom   D. Never

Identity Scorecard

1. Answer: A=5   B=4   C=3   D=2   Points: _____

2. Answer: A=5   B=4   C=3   D=2   Points: _____

3. Answer: A=2   B=3   C=4   D=5   Points: _____

4. Answer: A=2   B=3   C=4   D=5   Points: _____

5. Answer: A=5   B=4   C=3   D=2   Points: _____

6. Answer: A=5   B=4   C=3   D=2   Points: _____

7. Answer: A=2   B=3   C=4   D=5   Points: _____

8. Answer: A=5   B=4   C=3   D=2   Points: _____

9. Answer: A=2   B=3   C=4   D=5   Points: _____

10. Answer: A=2   B=3   C=4   D=5   Points: _____

Total points: _____

If your score was . . .

40–50: You are evidently secure in your identity and have a good support system of family and friends who have equipped you to know that you were created by God and that you have a purpose in life. You may enjoy hobbies and activities, but you are not defined by what you do or what you are good at. You are aware that if Jesus Christ is your Savior, your eternity is secure in Him.

30–39: You might want to take some time to consider yourself as a human *being* rather than a human *doing*. When we identify ourselves by what we do instead of who God made us to be, we run the risk of having an identity crisis when we can no longer do the things we once did. The Bible tells us in Matthew 7:15-20 that we are known by our "fruit"—not only by what we do with our lives but also by how we show forth God's love and nature.

20–29: It's never too late to understand that you can have an identity that is secure in Jesus Christ. He is a Rock who loves you unconditionally, who never changes, and who will never forsake you or leave you alone. He invites all people to come to Him just as they are. God has given each of us gifts and made each of us uniquely and wonderfully. By spending time worshiping Him and learning His word, we can learn what our gifts are and the purpose He has for our lives.[1]

Skills, Personality, and Spiritual Gifts

Understanding your skills, personality, and spiritual gifts will help you to recognize your personal identity and purpose at a greater level. This, in turn, enables you as a couple to discover where the natural intersections are between you in order to identify your mission and vision as a couple. Let's look at a few of them here.

Skills—What am I good at? What do people compliment me on doing? What do people look to me for?

Look for how and where your skills match certain occupations. For example, a skill with making numbers line up could lead to a degree in engineering or accounting. Or maybe you have a skill of bringing comfort to people that could point you in the direction of counseling, psychology, or serving in a church. Try to find where both your skills and your passions intersect to see what types of occupations fall in that category.

Personality—Do I like to be with people, or do I prefer to spend time alone? Am I a go-getter, or am I more cautious? Do I enjoy leading or following? Do I work better on tasks by myself or with other people in groups?

Your personality is a great indicator of what you were designed to do, because God has already prepared you for His purpose for you. Has He given you a personality that loves to be with people and talk all of the time? If so, then look where those traits line up with different purposes in life such as teaching, counseling, speaking, or pastoral ministry. Your personality can help you determine what will be the best fit for you long-term in a career and in your relationships.

Background—What have I experienced that is unique? Have I gone through any learning opportunities that have given me a head start in a certain area? How has my home life shaped who I am?

You may have a fairly normal background, but even in the most normal of backgrounds, there are things you have experienced or seen that have made you who you are. It could be that the very stability and normalcy of your background has equipped you for a purpose of bringing stability and normalcy into situations that might not have them, such as counseling or leading. Look at the experiences you have had to help you understand what God has purposed for you to do with your life.

When you line up your passions, skills, personality, and background and see where they intersect, you are on your way to discovering your purpose. When you identify your purpose individually, you are closer to discovering your shared purpose as a couple. It could be that your shared purpose as a couple is in supporting and encouraging each other to pursue and live out your individual purposes as well.

Spiritual Gifts Assessment

A great way to start discovering your spiritual gifts is to take a test called a Spiritual Gifts Inventory. Here's one based on an exam by Focus on the Family counselor Tim Sanford.[2]

Work through all seven lists. Mark with an "XX" any statements that seem to fit you *well*. Mark with a single "X" the statements you think *may* fit you. Some of the statements have a negative tone. Those don't describe the gift itself but rather the personality of someone in whom that gift is often found.

When you've gone through all seven lists, add up the statements you marked on each list and enter that number at the end of the list. Give yourself one point for each statement, whether you marked it "XX" or only "X."

You'll probably find that one or two lists have more statements marked than do the others. Those lists may indicate your spiritual gift(s). Don't be surprised if more than one list has lots of marks. You may have what's called a primary gift and a secondary one.

LIST ONE

_____ You're very good at stating the truth.
_____ You're bold when you relate to others—maybe even frightening at times.
_____ You talk straight, and your standards are straight.

_____ You tend to use Scripture to back up what you say.

_____ You often can identify what's evil.

_____ You're able to tell a lot about people's motives and character.

_____ You want to confront other people's selfishness and stop it.

_____ When others say they've changed, you want to see proof—not just words.

_____ You're direct, honest, and persuasive.

_____ Feelings don't matter as much to you as choices, facts, and truth do.

_____ You'd rather confront than just "relate."

_____ You tend to be better at talking than listening.

_____ You want to proclaim truth and let people know what will happen if they reject it.

_____ You don't compromise with sin.

_____ You have a strong sense of who you are.

_____ You have a strong sense of duty.

_____ You're concerned that people respect God and understand His character.

_____ You don't particularly care what others think of you.

_____ You have strong opinions, and may be stubborn.

_____ You're willing to be the "underdog."

_____ You can't stand it when people don't practice what they preach.

_____ You're more likely to be depressed than lighthearted about life and its problems.

_____ **Total number of statements you marked out of 22**

LIST TWO

_____ You really want to meet people's physical needs.

_____ You understand the practical needs of individuals and the church.

_____ You can recall people's specific likes and dislikes.

_____ You care about the details of what needs to be done.

_____ You find it hard to say no when something needs to be done.

_____ You tend to get involved in too many things.

_____ In focusing on others' physical needs, you may overlook their deeper needs.

_____ You expect everyone to be as dedicated and energetic as you are.

_____ You want to get the job over with so you can get to the next one.

_____ You want your help to be sincerely appreciated, and can tell when a "thank you" isn't heartfelt.

_____ You're preoccupied with the goal in front of you.

_____ You have a lot of physical stamina.

_____ You're willing to sacrifice, and want to get others to do that too.

_____ You're often more concerned about getting things done than about getting along with others.

_____ You tend to have a low self-image.

_____ When you run out of time, you're frustrated because you can't do that extra little bit.

_____ You're usually easygoing.

_____ You're loyal.

_____ You listen to others without criticizing them.

_____ You don't talk a lot in public.

_____ You're comfortable with letting others be in charge.

_____ You can put up with people who might irritate others.

_____ **Total number of statements you marked out of 22**

LIST THREE

_____ You're good at communicating in an organized way.

_____ You like helping others learn.

_____ You insist on using words accurately.

_____ You like arranging facts in a simple way so others can remember them.

_____ You believe that without teaching, the Christian faith would fall apart.

_____ You like to quote the Bible and other sources to support what you say.

_____ You tend to be more theoretical than practical.

_____ You really love learning and studying.

_____ You test the knowledge of those who teach you.

_____ You have to know the source before accepting new information.

_____ You resist using Bible verses or stories in ways they weren't meant to be used.

_____ It's easy for you to become proud of your knowledge and insight.

_____ You do your own investigating to find out what's true.

_____ If you're teaching, you sometimes rely on your own ability instead of on God's help.

_____ You'd rather analyze information than relate to people.

_____ You're creative and imaginative.

_____ You're more objective (facts, figures) than subjective (feelings).

_____ You like researching truth more than presenting it.

_____ You're self-disciplined.

_____ You explain things with authority.

_____ You make decisions based on facts.

_____ You tend to talk more than listen.

_____ **Total number of statements you marked out of 22**

LIST FOUR

_____ Nearly everything you do is practical.

_____ You get painfully bored hearing about theories.

_____ You really believe that what's humanly impossible is possible with God.

_____ You can visualize what a person could become through God's love.

_____ You love having conversations that help you see things in a new way.

_____ You tend to see trouble as a chance to grow.

_____ You really want your listeners to accept you and to approve of what you say.

_____ You like helping others solve their problems.

_____ You sometimes quote Bible verses out of context to make your point.

_____ You keep trying to make your point as long as others listen.

_____ You aren't satisfied until you've shown how to live out a truth in everyday life.

_____ It's hard for you to accept failure.

_____ You may write off those who cause you to fail.

_____ You find success exciting.

_____ You tend to give people advice instead of just befriending them.

_____ You tend to care more about getting results than about the other person's felt needs.

_____ You usually find it easy to talk in a group.

_____ You're more impulsive than self-disciplined.

_____ You're able to emotionally identify with others.

_____ You're more subjective (feelings) than objective (facts, figures).

_____ You tend to avoid formal ways of doing things if you don't see the point.

_____ You're motivated by a positive reaction from your audience.

_____ **Total number of statements you marked out of 22**

LIST FIVE

_____ You insist that people follow the rules.

_____ You sometimes make enemies when others think you're "using" people.

_____ You're confident.

_____ You're comfortable being a leader.

_____ You know how to delegate work to others.

_____ You can see the overall picture and long-range goals.

_____ You tend to wait on the sidelines until those in charge turn over the responsibility to you.

_____ You're good at organizing.

_____ You're able to sit quietly and listen before making comments.

_____ You're eager to complete a task quickly and get on to the next one.

_____ You'll put up with criticism from those you work with in order to reach your goal.

_____ You thrive on pressure—the more the better.

_____ You sometimes get so caught up in getting things done that you aren't sensitive to others' feelings.

_____ You like seeing the pieces of a plan come together.

_____ You're tempted to get back at others who treat you badly.

_____ You're good at details.

_____ You're thorough and careful.

_____ You make decisions based on facts.

_____ You care more about what's good for the group than you do about your own desires.

_____ You're more composed than nervous.

_____ You tend to accept others based on loyalty or ability to finish a task.

_____ You're more objective (facts, figures) than subjective (feelings).

_____ **Total number of statements you marked out of 22**

LIST SIX

_____ You give regularly and even sacrificially to your church and other ministries, no matter how much money you have.

_____ You make wise purchases and investments.

_____ You really believe in certain organizations that are trying to serve God.

_____ You want to have an active part in any cause to which you give.

_____ You carefully examine requests for your money.

_____ You want what you give to be of high quality.

_____ You refuse to be pressured into giving.

_____ You want your giving to motivate others to give.

_____ You want to avoid public recognition and give quietly.

_____ You want God to lead you in your giving.

_____ You get very upset when seeing others waste money.

_____ You're happy, even eager, to give.

_____ You make do with less in order to give quality to others.

_____ You may be good at earning money.

_____ You want confirmation by others you trust before giving.

_____ Your first thought when people ask for money is often "No."

_____ You have a pretty accurate view of yourself.

_____ You're more lighthearted than downhearted.

_____ You want people to like you.

_____ You're responsible.

_____ You love it when your gift is an answer to a person's prayers.

_____ You tend to be sympathetic.

_____ **Total number of statements you marked out of 22**

LIST SEVEN

_____ You're very sensitive to others' feelings.

_____ Your feelings can be easily hurt.

_____ You're very interested in people.

_____ You're drawn to people who are in distress.

_____ Healing and prayer are important to you.

_____ You're deeply concerned about people's inner struggles.

_____ You'll go to great lengths to help others.

_____ You find it tough to be firm with others.

_____ You tend to ignore those who don't have obvious needs.

_____ You have a hard time trusting others for fear of being hurt.

_____ You're tender and kind, and often express that by touching.

_____ You sacrifice to lessen others' pain and suffering.

_____ You can tell when you meet a person who's a "kindred spirit."

_____ You're turned off by people who aren't sensitive.

_____ You care more about feelings than facts.

_____ It's easy for you to get discouraged and say, "Poor me."

_____ You're inclined to have a low self-image.

_____ You're patient.

_____ You talk well with people, and they find it easy to talk to you.

_____ You can tell whether others are sincere.

_____ You're more subjective (feelings) than objective (facts, figures).

_____ When it comes to getting along with others, you can put up with a lot.

_____ **Total number of statements you marked out of 22**

Down to Earth

Take a look at the test you just took. Does one list have more marks than the others? If so, that may be your primary spiritual gift. Does a second list stand out above the remaining five? That may be a secondary gift.

If no list stands out, look over all the descriptions and see if one seems to fit you better than the rest. Keep in mind that other issues, including stress, may block your ability to see a spiritual gift—and could block a gift from being displayed at all. So be patient, and come back to this exercise later if necessary.

This test looks for what have been called the "seven motivational gifts" in Romans 12:3-8. Here they are:

LIST ONE: PROPHECY

If you have the gift of prophecy, you're probably highly sensitive to sin, to others' motivations, and to whether they're okay spiritually. This may not be too noticeable now, but it can become clearer as you mature. Being a prophet doesn't mean you have to hear God's audible voice talking to you; it means you're able to understand God's message and who needs to hear it.

LIST TWO: SERVICE

If you have the gift of service, you want to take care of the practical, physical needs of others. You're good at identifying unmet needs and helping church leaders meet them.

LIST THREE: TEACHING

With this gift, you have a passion for the truth and tend to make it clearer for others. You can communicate important information as a teacher or coach.

LIST FOUR: EXHORTATION

People with this gift are often seen as the encouragers or cheerleaders of a group. You can bring comfort and counsel to others.

LIST FIVE: ADMINISTRATION

If you have this gift, you like getting people to work together toward a goal. When you and your friends are planning a major activity, you're likely the one who gets everyone and everything organized—even if your friends think you're a little bossy in the process.

LIST SIX: GIVING

Yes, this is a real gift—though it often doesn't surface until a person is middle-aged. If you have this gift, you actually enjoy helping other people by giving away your money, possessions, and other resources. If you secretly want this gift in the hope that God will make you rich enough to give away more of your money, you probably don't have this gift.

LIST SEVEN: MERCY

The gift of mercy is not "feeling sorry" for people. If you have this gift, you have a strong desire to heal physical and/or emotional wounds. You feel compassion for hurting people and translate that into actions that show love and relieve suffering.

Other gifts may fall under the seven categories listed here. For example, the gift of hospitality could fall under the headings of either mercy or service. The gift of encouragement might fit under the category of exhortation.

Remember, this is not a scientific test with absolute answers. But it does give you a good starting point for considering what your spiritual gift(s) may be.

❖❖❖❖❖❖

COMMUNICATION AND CONFLICT TIPS AND ASSESSMENTS

COMMUNICATION. We all do it. We all mess it up from time to time. We all need it. Communication is a cornerstone of your relationship, and communication done well will be a hallmark of your marriage.

Let me ask you some questions to get started: Have you ever talked to someone and felt like you weren't heard? You saw their eyes glaze over or could tell that their mind was wandering off. Or when you were done, they just changed the subject. Do you remember how you felt when that happened? It hurts, doesn't it?

Or how about a time when you felt like you had communicated clearly what you were experiencing, but the other person just didn't seem to get it? Or worse yet, they got defensive and started turning the conversation around to defend themselves? (This is a common one.)

None of those times were times when healthy communication happened. Communication happens when one person speaks or shares information through nonverbal forms and the other person understands and responds accordingly. This doesn't mean that the other person has to agree, but that they understand and respond. It's called *validating*, and it goes a long way in healthy communication.

To *validate* simply means that you recognize the legitimacy of what was communicated. It comes out of a heart of respect for the other person. It is your way of saying that even if you don't agree, you respect that the other person feels the way they feel or views something the way they view it. You respect that they are entitled to their own opinion or perspective.

If you do disagree with someone, it's important to start out by validating what they said first. Something as simple as, "I hear you said _____, and that makes you feel _____, and I can understand how you might feel that way." Or "I don't understand why you feel that way, but I do respect that there is more information I may not know, so I don't want to jump to conclusions and judge you."

Follow up your validation of the other person with what you want to say. Doing this helps you communicate more effectively.

We all know what it's like to get spammed in text messages or on social media by someone we don't want to respond to. That is not a good way of communicating. So when you feel the urge to keep posting or texting when the other person hasn't responded, remember how that makes you feel when it's done to you. And remember that effective communication is always two-way. So be patient and wait. And let your fiancé know by how you communicate with him/her that you are a person who brings good to those around you.

Also, did you know that nearly 93 percent of all communication takes place through what is called *nonverbal* communication? That means you are talking without even talking. You are communicating through the way you walk, sit, stand, what you wear, whether you look people in the eyes or not, your gestures, posture—any number of things. Problems arise when we don't pay attention to what we are communicating nonverbally and we become lazy about it. Make sure to pay attention to what you are saying, even when you are not saying anything at all.

Here are some tips for good communication:

1. Make and maintain eye contact when talking.
2. Wear clothes that show you respect yourself and your future; dress with confidence.
3. Sit up straight; slouching indicates a lack of self-control and self-respect.
4. Listen and let the other person finish speaking before you begin.
5. Briefly repeat a one-sentence summary of what the other person said if you need to clarify before moving on.
6. Don't talk too long and dominate any conversation; let there be a balance.

7. Refrain from gossiping, slandering, and putting other people down. (It is not kind and it actually makes you look insecure.)
8. Don't talk too loud; be mindful of shared space.
9. Put your phone away when talking with your fiancé/spouse.
10. Be aware that if you get a phone call when you are speaking with your fiancé/spouse, you don't have to answer the phone. You can call the other person back after you finish your conversation.

Here are some tips to demonstrate respect through communication:

1. Giving value to their opinions and presence
2. Not interrupting someone when he or she is talking
3. Not being disagreeable just for the sake of disagreeing
4. Seeking to understand their perspective, even if it differs from your own
5. Not talking too loudly so as to draw attention to yourself
6. Being courteous and practicing the use of manners
7. Looking at the other person when they are talking to you rather than looking at your phone or tablet
8. Not dominating conversations or agendas
9. Not texting while driving (also a safety and legal issue)
10. Speaking well of yourself and not putting yourself down in conversation

Bear in mind that in all communication, there are three parts. The *encoder* is the person who wants to say something. The *message* is what's actually said. It's supposed to convey the encoder's intended information and emotion, but it has a life of its own and is easily misinterpreted. The *decoder* receives and deciphers the message to make sense of it.

If the decoder doesn't understand what was received, no matter how clear we (the encoder) thought we were, we may have to repeat ourselves. If our message is still not understood, we can sometimes get frustrated at the person listening.

1. Would you consider yourself a better listener (decoder) or talker (encoder)? Why? Give an example.

2. Why is decoding important in any conversation?

3. List five ways you can show you are listening to your fiancé.

4. Recall a time when you didn't feel heard by your fiancé. Could you have said something differently to have been heard? Share what that is.

Communication/Respect Assessment

For each statement, circle the letter next to the answer that best describes your interactions with others. Then follow the directions at the end of the activity.

1. When I work in a group, I listen carefully to what other team members say.

   A. Always

   B. Most of the time

   C. I usually check out.

   D. I don't have time for that.

2. I get upset when my team takes credit for my idea or action and I don't get recognition.

   A. Always

   B. Most of the time

   C. Seldom. It's meeting the goal that matters.

   D. Never. My ideas don't matter.

3. If one of my friends is offended, I am offended too.

   A. Always, and I let others know about it.

   B. Usually, and I let it affect how I treat the offender.

   C. Sometimes, but I try to help them reconcile.

   D. Never

4. If I am in conflict with someone, I make sure to avoid them whenever possible.

   A. Always

   B. Most of the time

   C. I do until I am ready to talk to them about the issue.

   D. Never. I stare them down or let them know they are wrong.

5. When I am upset with someone, I tell others about it to make myself feel better.

   A. Yes, especially if I know they will be on my side.

   B. Most of the time—I need to let it out.

   C. Seldom, or only with friends I trust to help me sort it out.

   D. Never. I keep things to myself and keep going.

6. When I am upset with someone, I check my attitude before confronting them about it.

   A. Always

   B. Most of the time

   C. Seldom; it's a lot of work to think about it.

   D. I am never wrong, and my attitude is justified.

7. If someone wrongs me, I am not satisfied until I have had a chance to get them back.

    A. True, the Bible says "an eye for an eye."

    B. It depends on what they did.

    C. Sometimes I feel that way but they'll get theirs in the end.

    D. I try to overlook and move on.

8. I sometimes pretend that things others say or do don't bother me, even when my feelings are hurt or I am angry.

    A. Yes, I do this often.

    B. Yes, with some people.

    C. Not really—I like to work it out.

    D. It's pretty hard to hurt my feelings.

9. If I am in conflict with someone, I check myself for what responsibility I might have.

    A. Always, conflict takes at least two.

    B. Most of the time

    C. Seldom or never—it is important to tell the other person what they did wrong.

    D. Seldom or never—I avoid conflict at all costs.

10. It is really important to resolve conflict and be at peace within myself and with others.

    A. Strongly agree

    B. Agree

    C. Disagree

    D. Strongly disagree

Communication/Respect Resolution Scoring Matrix

In the scoring graph below, circle the letter of your answer to show if you respond to conflict using Escape Responses, Attack Responses, or Peacemaking Responses.

Question	Escape Response	Attack Response	Peacemaking Response
1	C	D	A, B
2	D	A, B	C
3	D	A, B	C
4	A, B	D	C
5	D	A, B	C
6	C	D	A, B
7	C	A, B	D
8	A, B	D	C
9	D	C	A, B
10	C, D	C, D	A, B

Now, total the number of responses you have in each category and enter the number in the blank beside that category in the pie chart below.[2]

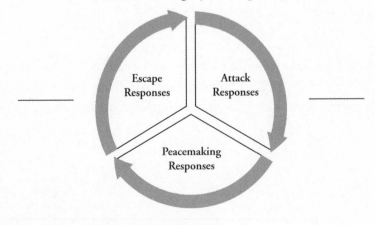

If your score was above 3 in the Escape or Attack categories, it is time to take a deep look inward and consider your role in conflict with others. Romans 12:17-18 advises us that we should not repay evil for evil, and that whenever possible, as far as it depends upon us, we should live at peace with all people. We are charged with the task of resolving conflict. On the other hand, while some offenses can be overlooked, others must be reconciled so that we don't harbor anger, pain, guilt, or other emotions that may build up until they reach a boiling point.

The following responses to conflict are adapted from the book *Resolving Everyday Conflict* and are used with permission from Peacemaker Ministries. Our goal is to be peacemakers and be respectful in our communication as a couple.

Escape Responses	Peacemaking Responses	Attack Reponses
Denial	Overlooking minor offenses	Assault
Flight	Reconciling through apology and forgiveness	Litigation (suing)
Suicide (the most extreme escape response)	Negotiation to find a position of compromise	Murder (the most extreme attack response)
	Mediation—having a third, neutral party help the negotiation	
	Arbitration—having a third, neutral party provide a solution that both parties agree to accept	

If you have fallen into habits of escaping or attacking, it will take some discipline to learn to be a peacemaker, but the rewards—inner peace, less stress and frustration, and peace with your partner—will be well worth it.

APPENDIX C

✠✠✠✠✠✠

EMBRACING ONENESS
THROUGH SERVING

SOME VOLUNTEER OPPORTUNITIES require forethought and orientation before you can actually serve together. You may want to look at the serving opportunities ahead of time and organize a way that you can serve as you go through this course. There are different ideas given and you can adopt one, some, or all. The purpose is to work together in a capacity that brings others good. This is one of the fastest ways to develop oneness.

These serving opportunities can be done with family members, neighbors, in your community, or also through your church. You may want to speak with your pastor or associate pastor who can help identify members in need. Discover personality and character qualities about your fiancé (and also about yourself) through these times of bonding and team-building activities. Be sure to discuss what you learn about each other during your lessons in this workbook, in casual conversation, or on a date.

Let's briefly look at the spiritual perspective of service before going through the serving options.

1. A Spiritual Mind-set of Service

Serving comes in a variety of forms. It could mean doing something for others or just encouraging them with what you say. It arises out of a heart that esteems others as valuable and makes it easier for them to deal with whatever situation they are in. It might be as simple as picking up an extra lunch for a coworker when you go through a drive-through, or it could be as detailed as helping your fiancé with a parking-lot trash pickup one Saturday morning or even going on a mission trip to help those who don't have clean water or enough food.

The Jesus who came to give us life is the same Jesus who asks us to take up our cross daily. Service ought to be motivated by more than a desire to cross an item off a list; it ought to be a way of life—a *mind-set*.

In fact, God tells us the reason He created us was for service. We read in Ephesians 2:10:

> For we are His workmanship, created in Christ Jesus for good works,
> which God prepared beforehand so that we would walk in them.

You were created by God "for good works." So if you are ever standing around wondering why on earth you are here, you have your answer right there: *to do good*. A "good work" involves an action or activity that benefits others while bringing glory to God. Essentially, it's serving.

Whether that service comes in a onetime action like passing out Christmas presents to needy families or giving the mail carrier a bottle of water in the summer, or whether it is a more long-term commitment to the betterment of another—all service matters to God. Service is not based on feelings. It's based on simply doing what you were put here to do. You shouldn't serve *only when you feel like it*.

Let me ask you a question: What would you do with a refrigerator that *didn't feel like* getting cold, or a stove that *didn't feel like* getting hot, or a can opener that *didn't feel like* opening any cans? You would probably replace them with appliances that would work. You would have to conclude that the refrigerator, stove, and can opener simply didn't understand the reason they had been chosen to be in your kitchen.

You have a role to play in this world. An important role. And when you play it well, people will know that you are a person who can be counted on to bring good wherever you go. When you serve as a couple, you become a power-packed force for good—bringing glory to God, oneness to your relationship, and impact to others.

Keep in mind that there is a careful distinction that needs to be made concerning service. Service that is done with a right heart attitude is service that is done expecting nothing in return. It is offered in order that God might be glorified and others benefited. Doing something for someone else and then expecting them to do something for you in return is called business, not service. And while there is nothing wrong with doing business, you just need to understand that it is only service when it is done to glorify God and help someone else.

No matter how small or how big the action, when accompanied by the right spirit of service, God takes notice. He has created you for a life of greatness, and that greatness comes by walking the path of service. Open up the flow of His favor upon you as a couple by doing together what He has put you on earth to do: good works that bring Him glory and honor.

2. Sample Serving Options

Serving Together at an Elderly Center

Volunteering at a senior home is one way to build your relationship through pouring into the life of another. You can easily volunteer by locating any nursing home or hospice facility in your area, or by asking around if there are friends or family members who are shut-ins due to age.

Some of the things you can do—on top of talking and asking the elderly to share their stories with you—is to play board games, do crossword puzzles, play an instrument for them, or have them play or sing for you. Be sure to take some photos of your time together and get them printed and delivered to them at a later time. If you are volunteering for the first time at a nursing or hospice facility, you may want to ask to be paired with the person or persons who receive the least visitors. This will make your experience additionally beneficial. Be sure to spend some of your time in prayer with the person you are visiting.

Serving Together Cleaning Up a Church Parking Lot or Public Place

Choose a church or public place, such as a park or eating area, where you can spend some time together picking up trash that has collected in the parking lot and surrounding areas. Be sure to pack some gloves and enough bags for the entire space you plan to help clean up. You will want to get permission from the owner of the property before cleaning up. If this is something you do well together, you may want to add a few more locations to clean up as well.

Serving Together Through Praying Together

This service opportunity involves identifying people to pray for as a couple. These could be your pastor and his family, missionaries you know who serve overseas, family members, workmates, friends, the elderly, or those you may have met on other service opportunities. Take a set amount of time to pray for others. Pray that God will bless, protect, guard, and guide them. Pray that He will shower them with His wisdom, favor, and peace. You may want to reach out to them and let them know you are praying for them. Ask if they have anything specific for you to pray on their behalf.

Serving Together Through Spreading Cheer

Unforgiveness brings about bitterness and anger in people's lives. One way to combat these negative emotions is by bringing cheer and joy to others. Go to a nearby flower shop or grocery store that sells flowers. Buy several bundles of flowers and then look for people to give them to who are exiting the store. Agree upon who you think may need this moment of cheer, and give them the flowers together, saying you both just wanted to brighten someone else's day. Conclude your time by asking if you can pray with them or for them.

Serving Together by Doing Yard Work

Doing yard work, planting flowers, mowing lawns, or trimming trees is a great way to learn more about each other in the context of serving someone else. You can find a widow, single parent, or shut-in through your church who may need some yard work done, or you could simply offer to help a neighbor or family member.

Be sure to ask the person you are serving what they want done and when. Then schedule a time with your fiancé to spend a morning or afternoon taking care of someone's yard. Conclude your time by praying for the person you served.

Serving Together Through Sending Videos

Take a video of yourself with your smartphone in which you spend some time using words of edification for a friend, family member, boss, coworker, or someone else you know. You can let them know you were encouraged to send this video as part of your preparation for a kingdom marriage. Then take a few minutes sharing what you believe to be words that will encourage, inspire, feed, and build up this other person. Each of you will do this for one other person. Discuss what types of words will bring the most encouragement to others.

Serving Together by Showing Gratitude to Service Workers

Spend some time preparing some thank-you bags for service workers, whether they are your local policemen, firemen, or church Sunday school teachers. You get to choose who you thank. Create a bag of goodies together and focus on ways to help people feel cherished. Part of romance comes in the area of cherishing each other, so this week's service project will assist you both in recognizing ways to cherish others and to demonstrate that tangibly. Ask if you can pray with them or for them about anything specific.

Serving Together Through Hospital Visits

A great way to serve together is to visit your local hospital's children's ward. Many children have to spend long hours in a hospital, and there are volunteer activities you can do with them such as reading to them, playing games, or singing to them. Be sure to check in at the nurses' station to see what is an appropriate and allowable way to serve. You can also visit other areas of the hospital to serve the elderly or sick through a cheerful balloon, bouquet of flowers, or by offering to read to them. Ask if there is anything you can pray about for them or with them.

Serving Together Through Life-Giving

When a thorn pricks you, it typically produces blood. This is because a cut or a tear has happened in your skin. Thorns hurt, but when viewed through a spiritual lens, the thorns of life's disappointments can produce life. As a reminder of one of our lesson's principles, find a place where you and your fiancé can go to donate blood or plasma to a medical facility. Know that you will be giving life and strength to someone else when they use it.

Serving Together Through the Written Word

Expressing heartfelt appreciation to someone is a way to encourage both you and the other person. In this lesson's service project, think of someone who may have contributed to your life in a positive way, whether that is your pastor, a schoolteacher, a drama coach, your parents, a mentor—anyone who has positively impacted you. Take some time to handwrite a letter thanking this person for the investment they made in your life. Tell how you feel about them and what you hope to one day accomplish as a result of the love and care they poured into you.

Learn to be free with expressing your feelings, knowing that doing so brings joy and satisfaction to those who care about you. You can each read the other's letter and talk about how and why you chose to write to the person you did. Hand-deliver or mail your letters. If the person is no longer alive, take some time to reflect on his/her life, and then bury the letter and plant a memorial tree over it.

Serving Together Through Child Care

Offer to babysit for a couple who may need a night out or a day activity away from the children. Serving together by taking care of someone's kids will enable you to invest in the lives of others while also discovering qualities and attributes of each other's strengths.

Preparing a meal together for the children can also give you the opportunity to work together while multitasking in caring for the needs of young ones. Pay special attention to what works well between the two of you when you share in this one purpose of making the babysitting experience successful not only for the children, but also for the parents. Think of something special you can do for the parents of the children you babysit by pampering them with something they may not always have easy access to.

Serving Together in a Pet Shelter

Locate a nearby animal rescue center and look into ways that you can volunteer together. There are many things that animal rescue centers can use help with: cleaning out cages, walking the dogs, playing with the animals, feeding the animals, administrative help, and more.

You will discover things about each other through a shared volunteer experience that you may not notice through dating or conversation. Growing closer in a serving opportunity can bring out additional talking points for discussion and help you recognize strengths in your partner you may not have seen before.[1]

APPENDIX D

✦ ✦ ✦ ✦ ✦ ✦

BLENDED FAMILIES

Sighed Mayzie, a lazy bird hatching an egg:
"I'm tired and I'm bored
And I've kinks in my leg
From sitting, just sitting here day after day.
It's work! *How I hate it!*
I'd much rather play!
I'd take a vacation, fly off for a rest
If I could find someone to stay on my nest!"

If you've had toddlers in your home at all, you have probably read more than you care to of Dr. Seuss's books to them. You might have even inadvertently memorized some by now, simply by reading them so much.

Not typically known for including a moral to instruct, most of his books center on artfully combining silliness with language finesse. But not *Horton Hatches the Egg*, from which the above quote comes. In this book, a clever tale of parenting invites readers to look at the more essential components of this role. Components such as loyalty, consistency, gentleness, tenderness, strength, character, and kindness show up, revealing how the combination of these traits subsequently transfer the likeness of the parent to the child.

The elephant and his egg is a tale of a blended family. It begins with a lazy bird named Mayzie, who gives up on the hard work of parenting and finds an elephant to take her place. Horton, an elephant of his word, sits on the egg for months on end, repeating the now famous line:

I meant what I said
And I said what I meant. . . .
An elephant's faithful
One hundred percent.

Horton's home life with Mayzie's egg ends up challenging him in multiple ways and taking him to many unexpected places—ushering in hardships and even criticisms from his friends. Ultimately captured by hunters, stuck on a boat for a treacherous sea adventure, and finally placed in a traveling circus—Horton remains nested on the egg.

When the circus winds up in Florida, Mayzie—who has been selfishly vacationing there all along—spots her egg and decides to reclaim it, especially now that all the hard work has been done.

However, when the life in the egg emerges from the cracked shell, what it has grown into resembles the elephant, Horton. It has developed into an elephant-bird. Thus, Horton and his new baby are promptly returned to the jungle to happily live out their days, while Mayzie is punished for her laziness and irresponsibility.

It is a child's story yet carries an overtly adult message—successful parenting comes through diligence, dedication, love, and hard work, also ushering in a lifetime of rewards.

The family unit in our nation today isn't always comprised of biological children in the home. We often have now what we call blended families, where one or both parents are raising children that they did not originally produce. I'm very familiar with this because we have a blended family in our own daughter Chrystal's home. Yet while two biological parents may be ideal, the underlying foundation of healthy parenting isn't merely tied to genetics. Rather, it is tied to the kingdom principles of parenting illustrated for us through an elephant named Horton—loyalty, consistency, gentleness, tenderness, strength, character, and kindness.

Whatever your family makeup and whatever stage you are in, if you will apply the principles we are going to go over together, there is always hope for a truly kingdom home.

Horton isn't the only elephant with a moral to teach. In fact, we can learn a lot from a group of adolescent bull elephants that were in a zoo and had begun to act unruly. These elephants had reached an age where they experienced periods of high hormonal levels, resulting in their more aggressive behavior. Left unchecked, these adolescent bulls were on a path to becoming extremely dangerous—apt to go on a rampage at any time. But what the zookeeper and the scientists chose to do in order to address the situation was to reflect the natural environment from which the elephants came.

Shortly after adolescent bulls break away from the herd in the wild and begin to wander away from what has been a strong matriarchal presence in their lives, older bulls become their mentors. The adolescent bulls submit to the presence and the power of the older bulls among them. In fact, they learn how to direct their hormonal upswings in more responsible manners that are productive to the herd rather than destructive.

When the zookeeper introduced adult bulls into the living space of the adolescents, the result was exactly what had been anticipated. Where there had been chaos, there was now calm, as the role of fatherhood converged with the role of motherhood to complete the environment so that the young elephants got what they needed to live well.

While elephants can't always be compared to humans, the principles evident in their interactions reflect what psychologists observe in teenagers today. So many teenagers are living a life of chaos simply because they are lacking the involvement and dedication of one or both parents. Parenting is so essential to the development of a boy into a man and a girl into a woman that many, if not most, of the issues that plague us as a nation today would be eradicated if we would just master this one thing. Rather than looking to the White House to fix all of our ills, we ought to be looking to our own houses to do just that. As goes the family, so goes the nation.

When the family breaks down, everything that's supposed to be built on that sacred foundation crumbles with it. And so God's kingdom on earth (made up of the body of Christ) is now reaping the devastation of family disintegration. When parents neglect to develop their children with the tools necessary to resist culture's onrush, the rising tide of secularism washes away a generation of children like sand castles on the shores of life.

A child's development is so critical that, in biblical times, whenever a young boy was earmarked to become a king later in life, many people took much care in training that boy how to be a king. Yet somewhere along the line, we have come to believe that the princes and princesses in God's kingdom don't need any significant training at all. Just as we saw in the illustration of the elephants, parental modeling and involvement impact the young. We see this impact show up in the life of a man many of you may have never heard of before, Asher.

Asher's Blended Home

Hidden in the somewhat tedious pages of 1 Chronicles—among the myriad names after unpronounceable names after names—lies one of the greatest examples of kingdom parenting that we have. His name was Asher, which in Hebrew means "happy." In chapter 7 of 1 Chronicles (as well as in Genesis 46:17), we read the genealogy of his descendants. It starts with his five children—four boys and a girl. As the only girl in the group of kids, no doubt his daughter, Serah, held a special place in Asher's heart. We know this for a number of reasons.

It is said in Jewish rabbinical literature that Serah is actually Asher's stepdaughter, thus making Asher a father of a blended home. She was the daughter of a woman named Hadurah, who had become a widow early on. History records that Hadurah married Asher when Serah was just three years old, and that he raised her as his own.

So loved and welcomed into the family was Serah that she is the only granddaughter mentioned in the entire lineage of Jacob, her grandfather. History records that it was Serah's tremendous piety and virtue that won her such a high place of honor in her adoptive family.

This same piety and virtue, though, was not something Asher could have claimed for himself when he was a young man, although he later went on to live a life accented with great wisdom. In his youth, Asher did something that was terribly wrong by anyone's standards. He joined in on a selfish and hardhearted scheme to have his halfbrother, Joseph, thrown into a pit and later sold as a slave to a traveling caravan headed to Egypt.

Perhaps due to his own early misdeeds and the ensuing guilt as he watched his beloved father grieve, as well as the subsequent near-starvation of his people at the start of the seven-year drought, Asher became a changed man. Maybe it came through witnessing Joseph model a spirit of character, mercy, and grace to him and his family. We'll never know for sure what brought about his transformation, but what we do know for sure is the legacy he ended up leaving behind. It is a legacy of great wisdom, blessing, character, and service to his nation at large. A legacy attached not only to him, but to generations of his descendants as well.

Asher's legacy ought to give each of us hope, especially those who may not have started out on the best possible footing as parents. Asher made mistakes early on—big ones that harmed his original family. He certainly didn't have it all together. In addition, he was raised in one of the most historically dysfunctional homes ever to be recorded biblically. Sprinkle on top of that the added burdens of a blended family of his own while married to a woman who had been married once before, and most might not have expected Asher to produce anything lasting at all.

But he did. In fact, his is a great legacy and a model for kingdom parenting today.

That legacy is recorded for us in 1 Chronicles 7, where we read, "All these were the sons of Asher, heads of the fathers' houses, choice and mighty men of valor, heads of the princes. And the number of them enrolled by genealogy for service in war was 26,000" (verse 40). According to Jewish legend, Serah went on to perform her own conquests as well.

No wonder Asher was a happy man. He did not look at his five children as getting on his last nerve. Rather, he was a satisfied man with an intention for his offspring and those brought in under his care. As a result, he and his descendants truly lived out the blessing given to him by his father: "Of Asher [Moses] said, 'More blessed than sons is Asher; may he be favored by his brothers, and may he dip his foot in oil. Your locks will be iron and bronze, and according to your days, so will your leisurely walk be'" (Deuteronomy 33:24-25).

Raising Leaders

The first parenting principle that we learn from the life of Asher comes from the verse where we learn that his sons were the "heads of the fathers' houses." Asher raised his sons, and also his daughter, to be leaders. They weren't just in the house, eating the food in the house, and taking up space around the house. According to the passage, these men grew up to fulfill a leadership role. In the Bible, "headship" refers to a leadership position within a home. Asher took his role as the head of his home seriously and subsequently raised up leaders over their own homes as well.

As a leader, Asher and his sons set the tone and direction for their homes and ensuing generations. One of the worst things that can happen to a family is to have parents who will not adequately fulfill their leadership roles. They want to be called parents without the commitment of parenting. Yet "headship" in the Bible isn't a title; it's a responsibility. So in order to claim the title, you also need to own the responsibility that goes along with it.

I can't say that I want to be a preacher and not want to preach. I can't say that I want to be a pastor and not want to give my church any leadership. That would be taking a title and misusing it. Likewise, parents need to fulfill the responsibilities that come within their realm, and they need to raise their children to do the same.

Secondly, Asher raised his children to excel in all things. We discern this from the descriptive terminology used to introduce them to us. It is written that they were "choice" men. Keep in mind that it was rare in historical Jewish culture to record much of anything about women, so based on the other writings already referenced, we can discern that Serah grew to be a choice lady as well.

By pointing out that Asher's descendants went on to become "choice" men, we know that these individuals grew up to become top of the line in all that they did. Asher and his wife raised choice children, those of high ethical character who were willing to accept and live out their responsibilities. They held high standards that wouldn't allow them to settle for mediocrity.

These were not children just trying to make it and get by, still living with Mom and Dad long after they were physically able to work and provide for themselves. Neither were these young adults postponing the responsibilities of life as long as possible by pursuing degree after degree after degree. Asher didn't raise his children to be like that. Rather, he raised them in a spirit of excellence and integrity—not having a perfect track record himself, as we have seen with the betrayal of his brother Joseph, but obviously seeking to steer his children onto a higher plane than even he had experienced.

Kingdom parents, if you are satisfied with your kids being mediocre, then mediocre is what you are going to get. Not only that, but they will one day grow up to marry someone else who is mediocre because mediocre is what they will know and understand. Rather, Asher raised his children to be the cream of the crop—to aim for excellence in all things. We know this because the entire community records their reputation in their genealogy as choice men.

It amazes me today how, in a room that is crowded and with no more seats available, men will allow women to stand for an inordinate amount of time and not even budge. My father would have knocked me off my rocker if I had ever let a woman stand for an extended period of time while I sat. But we've got a generation of children being raised without the simplest notions of etiquette, common courtesy, respect, honor, excellence, integrity, and more. This is because we have a generation of parents who are so distracted by the sights, sounds, and smells of life's adventures that they decide to simply settle for mediocrity in both themselves and their offspring. It's easier that way. But keep in mind that trifling children typically grow up to become trifling adults.

Now, it's true that not everyone is going to excel at everything. By raising kingdom kids who are choice, it simply means that they will be maximizing their potential and God-given gifts. Maybe they won't be in the top of their particular class in every subject, but whatever it is that God has created them to fulfill, they will do that with a degree of excellence, and they will do all else to the best of their abilities.

Thirdly, we learn from the text that Asher raised warriors. According to verse 40, he raised "mighty men of valor." What that describes is a person who is brave, courageous, and willing to risk himself for the betterment of the whole. *Valor* means boldness. It refers to someone who is willing to take a stand when a stand needs to be taken. These were children who grew into adults of conviction.

Too many of our children today crumble under the pressure of their peers rather than rise above the fray. They are indecisive, taking a stand for little or nothing at all. To raise up kingdom kids, you must instill in them a heart of valor—a spirit that will stay strong despite the challenges and enemies that may surround them on any given day. Scripture tells us that Satan roams around like a hungry lion seeking someone to devour. A kingdom kid must possess the knowledge and wisdom to be equipped for the spiritual battle that surrounds him or her. Asher raised children who could handle that.

Lastly, the passage tells us that Asher raised children who would serve others. They became mentors. We read that they were "heads of the princes." Essentially, Asher mentored leaders who were then positioned to influence the kingdom as mentors themselves. A prince is a king waiting to happen. By influencing princes, Asher's children influenced society.

They not only took care of themselves ("choice and mighty men"), their own homes ("heads of the fathers' houses"), and their own community ("mighty men of valor"), but they also took care of their country ("heads of princes"). Asher raised kingdom kids who understood that the stability and advancement of the kingdom began with themselves, woven through their families into their congregations and communities while ultimately impacting their nation.

Unfortunately today, many parents have lost sight of the long-term impact their children will one day make. As a result, some parents spend more time training their dogs than they do their kids. They never play with them, have Bible study with them, lead them to church, discuss what was taught, correct them when they are wrong, give them a vision and a dream, develop their character, instill Godly virtues, and so on. They don't do any of these things—or they do them halfheartedly—and then wonder why their children turn out the way they do. Rather than obtaining the generational cycles of victory like Asher and his wife experienced, they wind up with generational cycles of collapse passed on from their kids to their grandkids and so on. Instead of positive patterns being transferred, they transfer a DNA of defeat.

The passage we've been looking at in this chapter concludes with this summary of successful parenting: "And the number of them enrolled by genealogy for service in war was 26,000 men." Keep in mind that Asher started with only four boys and a girl. Yet by the time those five children raised their own families, who in turn raised their own families and this cycle continued, he produced a legacy of 26,000 choice men of valor, not counting the women of valor who were undoubtedly part of his tribe as well.

One of the greatest things that my father instilled in me as a child growing up in the middle of a country torn by racial disparity and injustice was that I was not primarily to identify myself by my ethnicity, but rather by my *citizenry*. As a citizen of heaven and a child of the King, I was taught to remember that I had royal blood flowing through my veins. If people called me names or didn't treat me justly, he would remind me that it wasn't a reflection of who I was. It was just a reflection of what they failed to realize—that I was a prince in God's kingdom.

Parents, there are a world of princes and princesses in our nation today who have no one to let them know it like my father did for me, or like Asher did for his four sons, stepdaughter, and subsequent grandchildren. There is no one to have Bible study with them, lead them to church, correct them when they are wrong, teach them about life and how to treat a girl or a boy, and what it means to be responsible and make wise decisions. What this has resulted in is a form of spiritual castration on the part of our young men and barrenness on the part of our young women. Their royalty has been ripped from them by a culture that fails to recognize them as a prince or princess at all.

What our nation needs today are men and women who will rise up to fulfill the high call of kingdom parenting. Parents who will act like a police escort, guiding their children safely into the future as they oversee the covenantal transference of the faith. Parents who will walk with them along the checkerboard of life until they finally reach the destination where each child can stand tall and say, "Crown me."

And then repeat the same cycle in their own home.[1]

✤✤✤✤✤✤

SAMPLE
BUDGET TEMPLATE

HOME BUDGET TEMPLATE

Monthly income for the month of: _____

Item	Amount
Salary	
Spouse's salary	
Dividends	
Interest	
Investments	
Reimbursements	
Other	
Total	

Monthly expenses for the month of _____

Item	Amount
Mortgage/rent	
Car loan	
Car insurance	
House insurance	
Life insurance	
Child care	
Charity	
Gas/electricity	
Telephone	
Cable	
Internet	
Food	
Pet supplies	
Health care	
Entertainment	
Gifts	
Clothing	
Other	
Total	

INCOME VS. EXPENSES

Item	Amount
Monthly income	
Monthly expenses	
Difference	

Please visit go.tonyevans.org/Christian-free-ebook-financial-victory? for a free download of the e-book *30 Days to Financial Victory*.

APPENDIX F

❖❖❖❖❖❖

NOTE TO MENTORS

CHANCES ARE, you have turned to this appendix because you're about to enter a mentoring relationship with another couple using this premarriage workbook. Good for you! As marriage mentors, you have a unique opportunity to support and strengthen this couple in their love for, and commitment to, one another.

At Focus on the Family, we're here to assist you in doing just that. Along those lines, we created the Mentor Moment section in each of the thirteen lessons of *Preparing for a Kingdom Marriage* to serve as a springboard to help you enter into candid marriage-building conversations with your mentee couple.

These Mentor Moments explore key characteristics that we've identified as essential ingredients in creating lasting, thriving unions. These traits all have their origin in Scripture, so it is not surprising that research demonstrates that a genuinely thriving marriage is the result of practical progress in these key areas of marital life.

Lifelong commitment, shared spiritual intimacy, cherishing one another, healthy conflict management, and the rest are among the non-negotiables in building and sustaining a vibrant marriage.

How to Use the Mentor Moment

We've drafted the Mentor Moment content as a helpful tool, not a rigid program.[1] It's intended to kick-start conversations and shine a spotlight on key facets of marriage, but we encourage you to decide how to best make it work for you and your mentee couple.

You may want to address each question, pick and choose, or add questions of your own. It's also important to remain flexible. If your mentee couple wants to explore a different subject instead, we encourage you to set aside the scheduled topic and go with the flow. And all along the way, ask good questions, actively listen, and share from your own experience.

We recommend tackling a single topic per week, as you'll want to facilitate relaxed, in-depth conversations. If you know in advance you will be meeting fewer than thirteen times, we'd suggest asking your mentee couple which topics are of greatest interest to them and then proceeding accordingly.

Again, thank you for making this investment in another couple's marriage. We're confident your mentees will benefit from your encouragement and insight, and you may be surprised how much it enhances your own marriage in the process. May God bless each of you as you embark on this exciting and important journey together!

NOTES

LESSON 11: ROMANCE
1. Sheril Kirshenbaum, "Sealed with a Kiss—and Neuroscience," *Washington Post*, Dec. 26, 2010.

APPENDIX A: PURPOSE AND PERSONALITIES
1. The Purpose/Identity quiz on pages 106–109 is based on content provided by counselor/ psychologist Tim Sanford for Focus on the Family.
2. Joe White with Larry Weeden, *Wired by God* (Carol Stream, IL: Focus on the Family/ Tyndale House Publishers, 2004), 53–61. Used by permission.

APPENDIX B: COMMUNICATION AND CONFLICT TIPS AND ASSESSMENTS
1. Adapted from Tony Evans, *Kingdom Quest: A Strategy Guide for Teens and Their Parents/ Mentors* (Carol Stream, IL: Focus on the Family/Tyndale House Publishers, 2015), 74–77. Used by permission.

APPENDIX C: EMBRACING ONENESS THROUGH SERVING
1. Adapted from Tony Evans, *Kingdom Quest: A Strategy Guide for Kids and Their Parents/ Mentors* (Carol Stream, IL: Focus on the Family/Tyndale House Publishers, 2015), 53. Used by permission.

APPENDIX D: BLENDED FAMILIES
1. Adapted from Tony Evans, *Raising Kingdom Kids: Giving Your Child a Living Faith* (Carol Stream, IL: Focus on the Family/Tyndale House Publishers, 2014), 20–29. Used by permission.

APPENDIX F: NOTE TO MENTORS
1. The content in the Mentor Moment section of each lesson originally appeared in Dr. Greg and Erin Smalley, *Ready to Wed: 12 Ways to Start a Marriage You'll Love* (Carol Stream, IL: Focus on the Family/Tyndale House Publishers, 2015). Used by permission.

THE KINGDOM SERIES
FROM DR. TONY EVANS

MORE RESOURCES TO GROW YOUR FAITH AND FURTHER GOD'S KINGDOM!

KINGDOM MAN
978-1-58997-685-6

KINGDOM MAN
DEVOTIONAL
978-1-62405-121-0

KINGDOM WOMAN
978-1-58997-743-3

KINGDOM WOMAN
DEVOTIONAL
978-1-62405-122-7

KINGDOM WOMAN
VIDEO STUDY
978-1-62405-209-5

KINGDOM MARRIAGE
978-1-58997-820-1

KINGDOM MARRIAGE
DEVOTIONAL
978-1-58997-856-0

KINGDOM MARRIAGE
VIDEO STUDY
978-1-58997-834-8

RAISING KINGDOM KIDS
978-1-58997-784-6

RAISING KINGDOM KIDS
DEVOTIONAL
978-1-62405-409-9

RAISING KINGDOM KIDS
VIDEO STUDY
978-1-62405-407-5

KINGDOM FAMILY
DEVOTIONAL
978-1-58997-855-3

CP0845

Meet the rest of the family

Expert advice on parenting and marriage . . . spiritual growth . . . powerful personal stories . . .

Focus on the Family's collection of inspiring, practical resources can help your family grow closer to God—and each other—than ever before. Whichever format you need—video, audio, book, or e-book—we have something for you. Discover how to help your family thrive with books, DVDs, and more at **FocusOnTheFamily.com/resources**.

More Resources to Help You Thrive in Marriage and Life

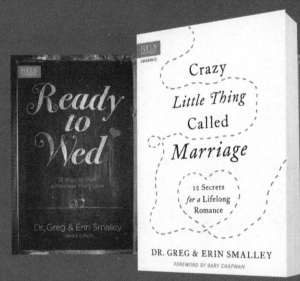

Starting now, this could be your best day, week, month, or year! Discover ways to express your needs, embrace your purpose, and love more fully. We offer life-transforming books, e-books, videos, devotionals, study guides, audiobooks, and audio dramas to equip you for God's calling on your life. Visit your favorite retailer, or go to **FocusOnTheFamily.com/resources**.